SOCCER

Steps to Success

Joseph A. Luxbacher, PhD
University of Pittsburgh

Leisure Press
Champaign, Illinois

Library of Congress Cataloging-in-Publication Data

Luxbacher, Joseph A.
      Soccer : steps to success / by Joseph A. Luxbacher.
          p.   cm. -- (Steps to success activity series)
      ISBN 0-88011-391-X
      1. Soccer.   I. Title.   II. Series.
      GV943.L87   1991
      796.334'2--dc20
                                                                        90-35489
                                                                        CIP

ISBN: 0-88011-391-X

Acquisitions Editor: Judy Patterson Wright, PhD
Developmental Editor: June I. Decker, PhD
Managing Editor: Robert King
Assistant Editor: Julia Anderson
Copyeditor: Barbara Walsh
Proofreader: Dianna Matlosz
Production Director: Ernie Noa
Typesetter: Kathy Boudreau-Fuoss
Text Design: Keith Blomberg
Text Layout: Tara Welsch
Cover Design: Jack Davis
Cover Photo: Wilmer Zehr
Illustrations: Raneé Rogers, Gretchen Walters
Printer: United Graphics

Instructional Designer for the Steps to Success Activity Series: Joan N. Vickers, EdD, University of Calgary, Calgary, Alberta, Canada

Leisure Press books are available at special discounts for bulk purchase for sales promotions, premiums, fund-raising, or educational use. Special editions or book excerpts can also be created to specification. For details, contact the Special Sales Manager at Leisure Press.

Printed in the United States of America

10   9   8   7   6   5   4   3   2   1

Leisure Press
A Division of Human Kinetics Publishers, Inc.
Box 5076, Champaign, IL 61825-5076
1-800-747-4457

UK Office:
Human Kinetics Publishers (UK) Ltd.
PO Box 18
Rawdon, Leeds LS19 6TG
England
(0532) 504211

Contents

Series Preface

The Steps to Success Activity Series is a breakthrough in skill instruction through the development of complete learning progressions—the *steps to success*. These *steps* help students quickly perform basic skills successfully and prepare them to acquire advanced skills readily. At each step, students are encouraged to learn at their own pace and to integrate their new skills into the total action of the activity, which motivates them to achieve.

The unique features of the Steps to Success Activity Series are the result of comprehensive development—through analyzing existing activity books, incorporating the latest research from the sport sciences and consulting with students, instructors, teacher educators, and administrators. This groundwork pointed up the need for three different types of books—for participants, instructors, and teacher educators—which we have created and together comprise the Steps to Success Activity Series.

The *participant book* for each activity is a self-paced, step-by-step guide; learners can use it as a primary resource for a beginning activity class or as a self-instructional guide. The unique features of each *step* in the participant book include

- sequential illustrations that clearly show proper technique for all basic skills,
- helpful suggestions for detecting and correcting errors,
- excellent drill progressions with accompanying *Success Goals* for measuring performance, and
- a complete checklist for each basic skill for a trained observer to rate the learner's technique.

A comprehensive *instructor guide* accompanies the participant's book for each activity, emphasizing how to individualize instruction. Each *step* of the instructor's guide promotes successful teaching and learning with

- teaching cues (*Keys to Success*) that emphasize fluidity, rhythm, and wholeness,

- criterion-referenced rating charts for evaluating a participant's initial skill level,
- suggestions for observing and correcting typical errors,
- tips for group management and safety,
- ideas for adapting every drill to increase or decrease the difficulty level,
- quantitative evaluations for all drills (*Success Goals*), and
- a complete test bank of written questions.

The series textbook, *Instructional Design for Teaching Physical Activities*, explains the *steps to success* model, which is the basis for the Steps to Success Activity Series. Teacher educators can use this text in their professional preparation classes to help future teachers and coaches learn how to design effective physical activity programs in school, recreation, or community teaching and coaching settings.

After identifying the need for participant, instructor, and teacher educator texts, we refined the *steps to success* instructional design model and developed prototypes for the participant and the instructor books. Once these prototypes were fine-tuned, we carefully selected authors for the activities who were not only thoroughly familiar with their sports but also had years of experience in teaching them. Each author had to be known as a gifted instructor who understands the teaching of sport so thoroughly that he or she could readily apply the *steps to success* model.

Next, all of the participant and instructor manuscripts were carefully developed to meet the guidelines of the *steps to success* model. Then our production team, along with outstanding artists, created a highly visual, user-friendly series of books.

The result: The Steps to Success Activity Series is the premier sports instructional series available today. The participant books are the best available for helping you to become a master player, the instructor guides will help you to become a master teacher, and the teacher educator's text prepares you to design your own programs.

This series would not have been possible without the contributions of the following:

- Dr. Joan Vickers, instructional design expert,
- Dr. Rainer Martens, Publisher,
- the staff of Human Kinetics Publishers, and

- the *many* students, teachers, coaches, consultants, teacher educators, specialists, and administrators who shared their ideas—and dreams.

Judy Patterson Wright
Series Editor

Preface

Soccer is the favorite pastime of millions of people throughout the world. It is an exciting sport that provides many physical as well as mental challenges. To truly derive the greatest fun and enjoyment from playing soccer, you should prepare for the demands that the game will require of you. You will have to execute a variety of skills under the game-related pressures of restricted space, limited time, physical and mental fatigue, and opposing players. Although you don't have to be any particular size or shape to play soccer, you need a high level of fitness for successful performance. You may have to run several miles during the course of a 90-minute game. Understanding game tactics and strategies is also important. Your decision-making abilities will be constantly tested as you respond quickly to a variety of rapidly changing situations during play. Individual and team performance ultimately depend on each player's ability to successfully accept and meet these challenges.

Whether your orientation is purely recreational or highly competitive, you'll enjoy the game more as your performance improves. This book has been written to provide you with a step-by-step plan for developing soccer skills and game strategies. Progress through the steps to success at your own pace.

At the end of the journey you will be prepared to participate successfully in a game situation.

I would not have been able to complete this project without the help and support of a great many people. I would like to express my sincere appreciation to the following individuals: To Dr. Joan Vickers for her insight and expertise in giving me a basic understanding of instructional design for teaching physical activities; to Judy Patterson Wright and June Decker, my developmental editors, whose patience, suggestions, and good humor helped me to persist at the task; and to Betty Datig, University of Pittsburgh, for her willingness to copy and then recopy the various illustrations presented to the artists for sketching purposes. Very special thanks and appreciation are extended to Gail Ann Polkis, a very special woman in my life, whose help with the illustrations and overall support of my efforts made the project much more enjoyable. I would also like to thank Kirsten and Grete, my nieces, for making me smile and for helping to keep things in perspective. Finally, and most importantly, I would like to thank my mother, Mary Ann Luxbacher, for her constant love and support in everything I do.

Joseph A. Luxbacher

The Steps to Success Staircase

Get ready to climb a staircase—one that will lead you to become an accomplished soccer player. You cannot leap to the top; you get there by climbing one step at a time.

Each of the 13 steps you will take is an easy transition from the one before. The first few steps of the staircase provide a solid foundation of basic skills and concepts. As you progress further, you will learn how to connect groups of those seemingly isolated skills. You will learn how to consistently pass and receive the ball, how to shoot, and how to play individual offense and defense. As you near the top of the staircase, you will become more confident in your ability to play as a team member, both offensively and defensively, and you will learn how to communicate effectively with your teammates.

Familiarize yourself with this section, as well as the "The Game of Soccer," and "Preparing Your Body for Success," sections for an orientation and in order to understand how to set up your practice sessions around the steps.

Follow the same sequence each step (chapter) of the way:

1. Read the explanations of what is covered in the step, why the step is important, and how to execute or perform the step's focus, which may be on basic skills, concepts, tactics, or a combination of the three.
2. Follow the numbered illustrations showing exactly how to position your body to execute each basic skill successfully. There are three general parts to each skill: preparation (getting into a starting position), execution (performing the skill that is the focus of the step), and recovery (reaching a finish position or following through to starting position).
3. Look over the common errors that may occur and the recommendations for how to correct them.
4. The drills help you improve your skills through repetition and purposeful practice. Read the directions and the Success Goals for each drill. Practice accordingly and record your scores. Compare your score with the Success Goals for the drill. You need to meet the Success Goals of each drill before moving on to practice the next one because the drills are arranged in an easy-to-difficult progression. This sequence is designed specifically to help you achieve continual success.
5. As soon as you can reach all the Success Goals for one step, you are ready for a qualified observer—such as your teacher, coach, or trained partner—to evaluate your basic skill technique against the Keys to Success Checklist. This is a qualitative or subjective evaluation of your basic technique or form, because using correct form can enhance your performance. Your evaluator can tailor specific goals for you, if they are needed, by using the Individual Program form (see the Appendix).
6. Repeat these procedures for each of the 13 Steps to Success. Then rate yourself according to the directions in the "Rating Your Total Progress" section.

Good luck on your step-by-step journey to developing your soccer skills, building confidence, experiencing success, and having fun!

KEY

X = Offensive player

O = Defensive player

X⊗ = Player with the ball

− − → = Path of the ball

⎯⎯→ = Path of player without the ball

⌇⌇⌇→ = Path of player dribbling the ball

S = Server

GK = Goalkeeper

SW = Sweeper back

STB = Stopper back

RB = Right back

LB = Left back

RMF = Right midfielder

CMF = Center midfielder

LMF = Left midfielder

RFW = Right forward (winger)

LFW = Left forward (winger)

CS = Central striker (forward)

The Game of Soccer

Historical accounts indicate that people have been fascinated with kickball-type games since ancient times. A forerunner of modern soccer was played in China as early as 2000 B.C. The Romans played a game called ''harpustum'' that was a combination of soccer and rugby. Participants from rival towns carried or kicked a ball from one village to the next—the ball was usually the inflated bladder of a cow or goat, and the town square the goal. These early games and their counterparts lacked uniform rules of play and only vaguely resembled soccer as we know it today.

Soccer gradually spread to Britain during the Middle Ages, when play was limited to the celebration of yearly festivals. British military troops soon adopted the sport as a favorite leisure pastime, and through the colonization efforts of the British empire in the 18th and 19th centuries it was introduced to many other parts of the world. Today soccer is the most popular team game in the world, with an estimated 22 million participants. Known internationally as ''football,'' soccer is the major sport of nearly every country in Asia, Africa, Europe, and South America. Soccer is presently enjoying tremendous popular growth in the United States as millions of youth players are participating in school- and community-sponsored programs. Many opportunities are also available for adult participation, and an estimated 3 million men and women are playing in amateur sandlot leagues throughout the country.

PLAYING THE GAME

A soccer match is played between two teams, each comprising 11 players, on an area that is longer and wider than the traditional American football field. A regulation game has two 45-minute periods. One player on each team is designated as a goalkeeper, who protects his or her team's goal. The goalkeeper can control the ball with his or her hands within the penalty area, an area 44 yards wide and 18 yards out from the endline. Field players may not use the hands or arms and must control the ball with the feet, legs, body, or head. The objective of the game is to score the most goals, which are earned by kicking or heading the ball into the opponent's goal. Each goal scored counts 1 point.

The alignment of field players can vary. Most systems of play deploy four defenders, three or four midfielders, and two or three forwards. Field players can move anywhere on the playing field, although each has specific responsibilities within the team's particular system of play.

A coin toss decides which team kicks off to start the game. Once play has begun the action is virtually continuous. The clock stops only after a goal is scored or at the discretion of the referee. Play is restarted after a goal by a kickoff at the center of the field by the team scored against.

RULES OF PLAY

The laws of the game* have been established by the Federation Internationale de Football Association (FIFA), the international governing body of soccer. Seventeen basic laws govern play on the soccer field. The FIFA laws are standard throughout the world and pertain to all competition between nations. (Minor variances in the substitution rules may occur in youth and school-sponsored programs here in the United States.)

Playing Field

Soccer is played on one of the largest playing fields of any sport (see Diagram 1). The field area must be rectangular with a length of 100 to 130 yards and a width of 50 to 100 yards. The length must in all cases exceed the width. (For international matches the length must be 110 to 120 yards and the width 70 to 80 yards.)

---

*The official FIFA rules can be obtained from the United States Soccer Federation National Headquarters, 1750 E. Boulder Street, Colorado Springs, CO 80909.

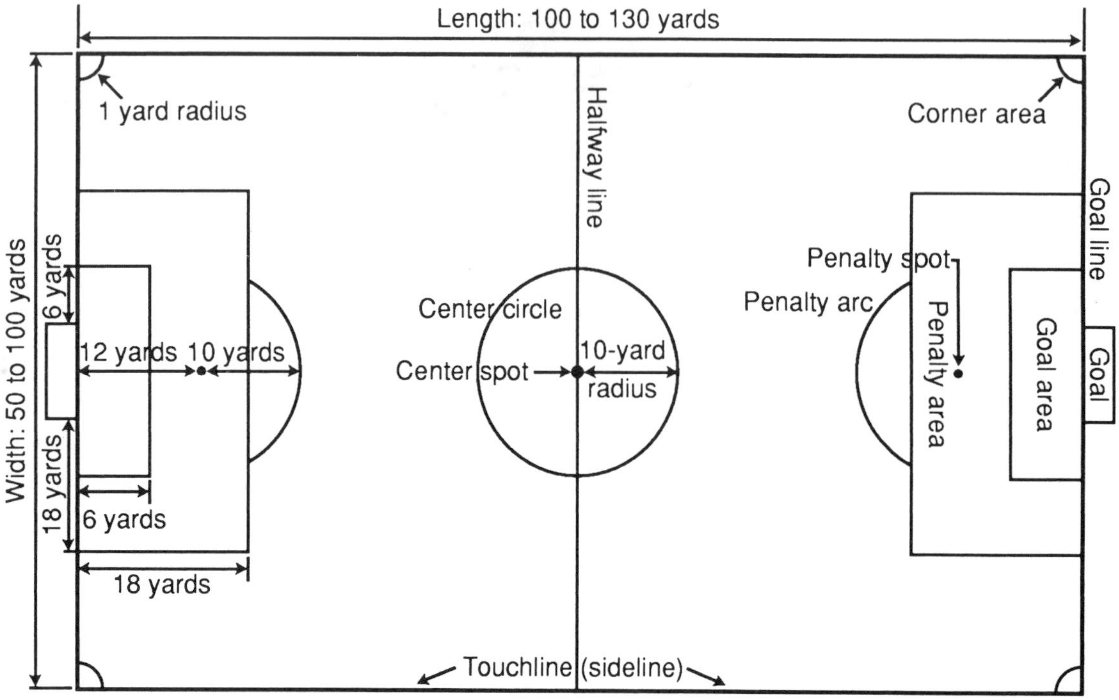

Diagram 1 Official soccer field.

The *field area* is marked with distinctive lines no more than 5 inches wide. The end boundaries of the field are called the *goal lines*, and the side boundaries are the *touchlines*. The *halfway line* divides the playing area into two equal halves. The center of the field is marked by the *center spot*, and a *center circle* with a radius of 10 yards is marked around it.

A *goal* 8 feet high and 24 feet wide is positioned at each end of the field on the center of the goal line. The *goal area* is a rectangular box drawn along each goal line. It is formed by two lines drawn at right angles to the goal line, 6 yards from each goalpost. These lines extend 6 yards onto the field of play and are joined by a line drawn parallel with the goal line.

The *penalty area* is a rectangular box drawn along each goal line, formed by two lines drawn at right angles to the goal line, 18 yards from each goalpost. The lines extend 18 yards onto the field of play and are joined by a line drawn parallel with the goal line. The *goal area* is enclosed within the penalty area.

Located within the penalty area is the *penalty spot*. The penalty spot is marked 12 yards front

and center of the midpoint of the goal line. Penalty kicks are taken from the penalty spot. The *penalty arc* line having a radius of 10 yards from the penalty spot is drawn outside of the penalty area.

A *corner area* with a radius of 1 yard is marked at each corner of the field. Corner kicks are taken from within the corner area.

Equipment and Attire

The soccer ball is spherical and made of leather or other approved materials. The official FIFA ball is 27 to 28 inches in circumference and weighs between 14 and 16 ounces. The regulation-size adult soccer ball is designated internationally as the Size #5 ball. Smaller balls (Size #4) are sometimes used for youth games.

The required attire for a field player consists of a jersey or shirt, shorts, socks, and shoes. Goalkeepers often wear shirts and shorts with padding at the elbows and hips. Players are not permitted to wear anything that the referee feels is potentially dangerous to another player. For example, watches, chains, and other jewelry are usually forbidden.

Officials

A referee is appointed to officiate each game. The referee enforces the laws of the game and has ultimate authority on the field. Two linesmen assist the referee in officiating a game. They are primarily responsible for signaling when the ball is out of play and for determining which team is entitled to the throw-in, goal kick, or corner kick. The linesmen also help the referee determine when offside violations have occurred.

Playing the Game

Play begins when a player takes a placekick from the center spot of the field. Opposing players must position themselves in their own half of the field at least 10 yards from the ball. The ball is not considered in play until it has traveled into the opponent's half of the field the distance of its own circumference. The kicker is not permitted to play the ball a second time until it has been touched by another player. The game is restarted in the same manner after each goal and also to begin the second period of play.

Out of Play

The ball is considered out of play when it has completely crossed the touchlines or goal lines, whether on the ground or in the air, or when the game has been stopped by the referee. The ball is in play at all other times from start to finish of the match, including

- rebounds from a goalpost, crossbar, or corner flag onto the field of play;
- rebounds off the referee or linesmen when they are in the field of play; and
- until a decision is rendered on a supposed infringement of the laws.

If the referee is unsure of who last touched a ball that traveled out of bounds, play is restarted with a drop ball at the spot where the ball was last in bounds. The referee drops the ball between two opposing players who cannot attempt to gain possession until the ball has first touched the ground.

When the ball travels out of play over a sideline (touchline), either on the ground or in the air, it is returned into play by a throw-in from the point where it left the playing field. A player from the team opposite to that of the player who last touched the ball takes the throw-in. The thrower must face the field of play with each foot touching the sideline or the ground outside of the sideline at the moment the ball is released. The thrower must hold the ball with both hands and deliver it from behind and over his or her head. The ball is considered in play immediately after it crosses the sideline onto the field of play. The thrower is not permitted to touch the ball a second time until it has been played by another player. A throw-in is awarded to the opposing team if the ball is improperly released onto the field of play. A goal cannot be scored direct from a throw-in.

A ball last touched by a member of the attacking team that passes over the goal line, excluding the portion of the line between the goalposts and under the crossbar, is returned into play by a goal kick awarded to the defending team. The goal kick is taken from a point within that half of the goal area nearest to where the ball crossed the goal line. The ball is considered in play once it has traveled outside the penalty area. The kicker cannot play the ball a second time until it has been touched by a teammate or an opponent. A goal kick cannot be played directly to the goalkeeper within the penalty area. All opposing players must position themselves outside the penalty area when a goal kick is taken. A goal cannot be scored directly off a goal kick.

A ball last touched by a member of the defending team that passes over the goal line, excluding the portion of the line between the goalposts and under the crossbar, is returned into play by a corner kick awarded to the attacking team. The corner kick is taken from within the quarter circle of the corner nearest the point where the ball left the playing area. Defending players must position themselves at least 10 yards from the ball until it is played. The kicker is not permitted to play the ball a second time until it has been touched by another player. A goal may be scored directly from a corner kick.

Scoring

A goal is scored when the ball has passed completely over the goal line between the goalposts and under the crossbar, provided it has not been thrown, carried, or intentionally propelled by the arm or hand of a player on the attacking team. Each goal scored counts as one point. The team scoring the greater number of goals during a contest wins the game. The game shall be termed a *draw* if both teams score an equal number of goals during regulation time.

Offside

It is important that all players be familiar with the offside law. A player is offside if he or she is nearer to the opponent's goal line than to the ball at the *moment the ball is played* unless

- the player is in his or her own half of the field;
- two or more opponents are nearer to their own goal line than the player in question;
- the ball was last touched by an opponent or was last played by the player in question; or
- he or she received the ball directly from a goal kick, corner kick, throw-in, or drop ball.

A player in an offside position should not be penalized unless in the judgment of the referee he or she is interfering with the play or with an opponent, or is seeking to gain an advantage from being in an offside position. The punishment for infringement of the offside law is an indirect free kick awarded to a player of the opposing team at the spot where the offside occurred. It is important to consider that the referee judges offside at the instant the ball is played and not at the moment the player receives the ball. A player who is onside at the moment the ball is played does not become offside if he or she moves into an offside position to receive the pass while the ball is in flight.

Free Kicks

There are two types of free kicks—*direct* and *indirect*. A goal can be scored directly against the opposing side from a direct free kick. To score from an indirect free kick the ball must be played or touched by a second player other than the kicker before passing over the goal line. When a player takes a free kick from within his or her own penalty area, all opposing players must remain outside the area and position themselves at least 10 yards from the ball. The ball must be stationary when the kick is taken and is considered in play once it has traveled the distance of its circumference and beyond the penalty area. If the kicker touches the ball a second time before it has been touched by another player, then an indirect free kick is awarded to the opposing team.

Opposing players must position themselves at least 10 yards from the ball when a player takes a direct or indirect free kick. The only instance in which defending players can be closer than 10 yards to the ball is when the attacking team has been awarded an indirect free kick within 10 yards of the defending team's goal. In that situation defending players can stand on their goal line between the goalposts in an attempt to block the kick from entering the goal.

Fouls

Fouls are generally categorized as either direct or indirect. A player who intentionally commits any of the following offenses will be penalized by the award of a direct free kick to the opposing team at the spot where the foul occurred:

- Kicking an opponent
- Tripping an opponent
- Jumping at an opponent
- Charging an opponent in a violent or dangerous manner
- Charging an opponent from behind unless the opponent is obstructing the player from the ball
- Striking an opponent
- Holding an opponent
- Pushing an opponent
- Carrying, striking, or propelling the ball with hand or arm (this violation does not apply to the goalkeeper within his or her penalty area)

If a player on the defending team intentionally commits one of these nine offenses within his or her own penalty area, the opposing team is awarded a penalty kick.

Indirect free kicks result from the following rule infractions:

- Playing in a manner the referee considers dangerous to you or another player
- Charging an opponent with your shoulder when the ball is not within playing distance of the players involved (charging with the shoulder is legal if you are attempting to play the ball)
- Intentionally obstructing an opponent when not attempting to play the ball
- Charging the goalkeeper except when he or she has possession of the ball or has moved outside the goal area
- When the goalkeeper takes more than four steps while in possession of the ball without releasing it
- Violation of the offside rule

Reprimands

It is the referee's discretion to reprimand a player who continually commits flagrant violations of the laws. The referee officially cautions a player by issuing a *yellow card*. A yellow card violation conveys a warning to the player that he or she will be ejected from the game if similar violations continue. The referee issues a *red card* to signal that a player has been ejected from the game. An ejected player cannot return to the game and cannot be replaced by a substitute.

Penalty Kick

The most severe sanction for a direct foul, other than ejection from the game, is the *penalty kick*. A penalty kick results when a player commits a direct foul within his or her team's penalty area. The kick is taken from the penalty spot. All players with the exception of the kicker and the goalkeeper must position themselves outside the penalty area at a distance of at least 10 yards from the penalty spot. The goalkeeper must stand on the goal line between the goalposts and is not permitted to move his or her feet until the ball has

been played. The kicker must kick the ball forward and cannot touch it a second time until it has been played by another player. The ball is considered in play once it has traveled the distance of its circumference. A goal can be scored directly from a penalty kick. Time should be extended if necessary at halftime or the end of regulation time to allow a penalty kick to be taken.

SOCCER TODAY

Soccer can truly be considered the sport of the masses. The modern game is characterized by fluid, controlled movement of players, each able to express his or her individuality within a team structure. Speed, strength, stamina, skill, and tactical knowledge are all important aspects of performance. The challenges confronting players are many and varied, which may be a primary reason that the game seems to have universal appeal. In a global society subdivided by numerous physical as well as ideological factors, soccer's popularity is not confined by age, sex, political, religious, cultural, or ethnic boundaries.

Tactics of team play have undergone many modifications during the evolution of the sport. In earlier times players filled very specialized roles. Forwards were expected to attack and score goals; defenders were given the sole task of preventing the opposition from scoring goals. Positional responsibilities were restricted with little overlap of roles. Today the game requires much more of players. Modern systems of play place a premium on the complete soccer player, one who can defend as well as attack. The days of the specialist are gone—today the philosophy of ''total soccer'' pervades the sport.

Because soccer is an international game, the rules and regulations must be standard throughout the world. FIFA functions as the governing body of world soccer. More than 140 nations, including the United States, presently hold membership in FIFA. The various professional and amateur associations in our country are organized under the auspices of the United States Soccer Federation (USSF) established in 1913. The United States Youth Soccer Association (USYSA) was established in 1974 as an affiliate of the USSF to accommodate the tremendous popular growth of youth soccer. The USYSA administers and promotes the sport for players under 19 years old.

The future of soccer in the United States appears very promising. Millions of young children are participating in recreational leagues throughout the country. The number of school-sponsored programs for boys and girls is also increasing. At the collegiate level more than 500 member institutions of the National Collegiate Athletic Association (NCAA) sponsor varsity men's programs, and nearly 200 colleges sponsor varsity women's programs. Many schools belonging to the National Association of Intercollegiate Athletics (NAIA) also field varsity teams. Opportunities exist for adults to play the game in the numerous sandlot leagues that have been organized throughout the country. A milestone in the history of American soccer will be reached in 1994 when for the first time the United States will host soccer's international championship, the World Cup tournament. Initiated in 1930, the World Cup is conducted every 4 years and is considered the world's most spectacular sporting event as nations throughout the world focus attention on the games.

The following organizations administer soccer competition in the United States. Collegiate competition for both men and women is controlled by the National Collegiate Athletic Association (NCAA), the National Association for Intercollegiate Athletics (NAIA), or the National Junior College Athletic Association (NJCAA). Amateur and professional soccer competition is under the direction of the United States Soccer Federation (USSF). Questions or requests for information should be directed to the appropriate governing body at the address listed here.

NCAA
Nall Avenue at 63rd Street
P.O. Box 1906
Mission, KS 66201

NAIA
1221 Baltimore Avenue
Kansas City, MO 64105

NJCAA
P.O. Box 7305
Colorado Springs, CO 80933

USSF
1750 E. Boulder Street
Colorado Springs, CO 80909

Soccer players are among the most physically fit of all athletes. A field player may be required to run more than 5 miles in a typical 90-minute game. Components of soccer-related fitness include flexibility or range of motion, agility, aerobic (cardiorespiratory) and anaerobic endurance, and muscular strength. Although fitness alone does not guarantee that you will become a good soccer player, without a sufficient level of fitness you cannot achieve your potential as a player. Train for the specific fitness demands of the soccer match. Whenever possible include a soccer ball in your training exercises, because skill execution is also an important component of soccer performance. Combining skill training and fitness training in a single exercise is an example of "economical training" that maximizes the use of practice time.

WARM-UP

Before every practice session perform a series of warm-up exercises that will physically and psychologically prepare your body for strenuous activity. Warm-up exercises function to elevate muscle temperatures and promote increased blood flow. This in turn improves your muscular contraction and reflex time, increases suppleness, and helps prevent soreness. Muscle and joint injuries are less likely to occur if training is preceded by a warm-up period.

"How long and hard should I warm up?" That is an issue of concern to all players. Because the needs of individuals vary there is no hard and steadfast answer to that question. As a general rule of thumb you should warm up for approximately 10 to 15 minutes at sufficient intensity to cause sweating. Sweating is an indication that your muscle temperatures are elevated.

Warm your muscles before performing flexibility exercises by promoting increased blood flow, something commonly called "getting your blood moving." To do so you must elevate your heart rate from the resting state. Choose one or more of the following exercises to get your blood moving. Then select one exercise for each body part from the flexibility exercises and strength exercises. Finally, select two exercises from the endurance exercises to develop your general endurance capacity.

Exercises to Elevate Your Heart Rate

1. *Dance on the ball*: Stand with a ball placed on the ground in front of you. Lightly touch the sole of your right foot to the top of the ball, then the sole of your left foot, then right, left, right, and so on. Your motion should look like you are going to step on top of the ball; however, as your foot touches the ball, quickly withdraw it and repeat the motion with the opposite foot. Alternate touches on the ball as fast as you can for 30 to 60 seconds.

2. *Inside-of-the-foot touches*: Stand with feet shoulder-width apart. Place a ball between your feet. Use the inside surfaces of your feet to tap the ball back and forth between your feet. Perform the exercise as fast as you can for 30 to 60 seconds. Rest, then repeat.

3. *Circle tag*: Play with a classmate within the center circle of the field. You are designated "it" to begin the game. Chase and attempt to tag your classmate. If you catch him or her the roles change and your classmate immediately becomes the chaser. Do not leave the circle to avoid being tagged. Play for 2 minutes continuously, then rest for 30 seconds. Repeat 3 times.

Flexibility Exercises

Flexibility exercises increase the range of motion around a joint or series of joints. Because soccer players must execute highly skilled movements while running with the ball, a restricted range of motion can be a limiting factor of performance. Static stretching is the preferred method for increasing your flexibility. Do not bounce or jerk when you stretch. Gradually extend the muscle or group of muscles until you feel the stretch and hold that position. The following exercises can be used to improve your flexibility. Choose one exercise for each body part.

Hamstrings

1. *Sitting hamstring stretch*: From a sitting position with one leg straight and the other bent 90 degrees, tilt your pelvis and gently lean forward. Try to keep your back as straight as possible. Hold the stretch position for 15 to 30 seconds, relax, and then repeat. Perform 2 repetitions.

2. *Bent leg stretch*: Lie on your back with your knees bent and your feet flat on the ground. Place your right hand behind your left ankle and your left hand behind your left thigh. Flex at the hip and pull gently on your calf until you feel a stretch. Pause for 15 to 30 seconds. After 2 repetitions, repeat using your right leg.

3. *Straddle leg stretch*: From a sitting position with legs spread no more than 45 degrees, lower your head toward your right knee, then repeat to your left knee. You should have a slight bend at the knee. Keep your back straight and your abdominal muscles tight. Hold each stretch for 15 to 30 seconds. Perform 2 repetitions for each leg.

Quadriceps

1. *Lying on side quad stretch*: Lie on your left side and support yourself on your left forearm. Flex your right leg and grab your right ankle with your right hand. Slowly pull the leg back until you feel a good stretch in your upper thigh. Be careful not to arch or hyperextend your back. Hold that position for 15 to 30 seconds, then repeat with the other leg. Perform 2 repetitions for each leg.

Calves and Achilles Tendons

1. *Wall lean*: Stand approximately 3 feet from a wall or a classmate. Place your feet parallel to each other several inches apart. Lean forward and use your outstretched hands to brace yourself on the wall or your partner. Keep your feet and heels flat on the floor as you lean forward. Hold that position for 15 to 30 seconds. Perform 2 repetitions.

2. *Lunge stretch*: Place both hands on your left knee for support. Bend your left leg 90 degrees and extend your right leg back with your heel off the floor. Hold the stretch position for 15 to 30 seconds, then repeat with the other leg. Perform 2 repetitions for each leg.

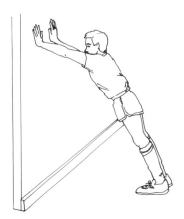

2. *Push-up position stretch*: Assume a normal push-up position. Place one foot on top of the heel of the other (balance) foot. Slowly push backward with your arms and try to touch the heel of your balance foot to the ground. Push as far as possible without pain and hold that position for 15 to 30 seconds. Do not let your body sag. Repeat 2 times with each leg.

3. *Lying on stomach quad stretch*: Lie on your stomach with your legs straight. Raise one leg until you feel a stretch. Hold for 15 to 30 seconds, relax, and then repeat with the other leg. Perform 2 repetitions for each leg.

Groin

1. *Sitting groin stretch*: Assume a sitting position with the soles of your feet touching in front of you. Place your hands on the inside

surface of your legs just above your knees. Use your hands to gently push down on the inside of your knees. Hold the stretch for 15 to 30 seconds, then relax. Perform 2 repetitions.

2. *Lying groin stretch*: Lie on your back. Flex your knees and place the soles of your feet together in front of you. Spread your legs as far as you can as you try to lower the outside area of each knee as close to the ground as possible. Hold the stretch for 15 to 30 seconds, then relax. Perform 2 repetitions.

Back

1. *Ball around feet*: Assume a sitting position with legs together and knees flexed. Slowly roll a soccer ball in a complete circle around your feet and your back. Try to keep both hands on the ball at all times. Repeat 10 times, then reverse direction for 10 repetitions.

2. *Standing lower back stretch*: Stand with your feet wide apart, your knees bent, and a soccer ball on the ground beneath you. Bend

forward at the waist, cross your arms, and try to touch one elbow on the soccer ball. Hold the stretch position for 15 to 30 seconds, then change elbows. Perform 2 repetitions for each elbow.

3. *Lying back stretch*: Lie on your back with arms extended to your sides. Slowly bring your knees up toward your chin as far as possible without raising your hands and arms off the floor. Lift your hips just slightly off the floor. Hold that position for 15 to 30 seconds, then relax. Perform 2 repetitions.

Neck

1. *Static neck stretch*: Use your hand to slowly push your head to one side; do not jerk! Hold the stretch position for 15 to 30 seconds, then relax. Repeat the stretch to the opposite side, then front.

2. *Head turns*: Turn your head as far as possible toward the right. Hold for 15 to 30 seconds, then turn to the left. Perform 2 repetitions in each direction.

Stength Exercises

The following exercises are designed to improve your muscular strength. Select one exercise for each body part.

Abdominals

1. *Abdominal curls*: Lie flat on the ground with your knees flexed and arms folded across your chest. Rise up slowly until your upper back is at approximately a 45-degree angle. Your lower back should remain on or near the ground. Lower yourself slowly to the ground and repeat. Do not perform this exercise with your hands behind your head or neck; in that position you may be tempted to pull on your neck. Perform 10 to 30 repetitions.

2. *Wall sit-up*: From a sitting position place your legs upward against a wall or a partner. Try to keep your legs straight as you sit up and touch your hands to your toes. Attempt 10 to 30 repetitions.

Legs

1. *Walk-ups*: Stand next to a bench about 12 inches high. Step up on the bench with one foot, then the other. Immediately step down with one foot, then the other, and repeat the exercise. Use a 4-count rhythm (e.g., up, up, down, down). Perform 20 repetitions, rest, then repeat.

2. *Marching*: March in place, bending your knees 90 degrees. Perform 50 repetitions with each leg.

3. *Over and back*: Stand beside a stationary ball. Keep your feet together as you jump over the ball from one side to the other. Be careful not to step on the ball. Stand slightly behind or in front of the ball if you have difficulty jumping over it. Repeat at maximum speed for 30 to 60 seconds, rest, then repeat.

Arms and Chest

1. *Knee push-ups*: Begin on your hands and knees with hands slightly more than shoulder-width apart. Lower your body straight down until your chest lightly touches the ground, then push yourself straight up to the starting position. Do not let your body sag. To develop your triceps place your hands closer together and keep your elbows close to your body. To develop your chest place hands farther apart. Perform 10 to 30 repetitions.

2. *Regular push-ups*: Assume a push-up position with your body weight supported by your arms and legs. Place your hands approximately shoulder-width apart with legs straight behind you. Slowly lower your body until your chest touches the ground, then use your arms to raise yourself to the starting

position. Do not let your body sag. Repeat 10 to 30 times, depending on your initial level of strength.

3. *Ball push-ups*: Assume a push-up position with your hands positioned on top of a soccer ball. Keep your legs straight with your body weight supported by your arms and toes. Slowly lower your body until your chest touches the ball, then raise yourself to the starting position. Do not let your body sag. Perform 5 to 20 repetitions depending on your initial level of upper body strength.

4. *Walking push-up*: Assume a push-up position with a ball in front of you. Support your body weight with your arms, chest, and toes. Walk forward on your hands as you nudge the ball with your forehead. Don't let your knees touch the ground or allow your body to sag. Walk forward in the push-up position for a distance of 20 to 30 yards.

Endurance Exercises

The following exercises will develop your general endurance capacity. Choose two exercises for your training session.

1. *Shuttle runs*: Place four cones in a straight line at distances of 5, 10, 15, and 20 yards from the goal line. You and a classmate take turns running the shuttle. Sprint to the first cone and back to the starting line, then to the second cone and back, to the third cone and back, and finally to the fourth cone and back. Complete the shuttle as quickly as you can. Rest while your classmate completes his or her turn. Repeat 4 to 8 times.

2. *Around the cone and back*: Place a cone 20 yards from the goal line. Stand on the goal line with a classmate. You begin the exercise by dribbling around the cone and back to the goal line as quickly as possible. Exchange the ball with your classmate who in turn dribbles around the cone and back to the goal line. Complete 5 to 15 repetitions each.

3. *Follow the leader*: You and a classmate each have a ball. Begin the exercise by dribbling your ball anywhere within the playing field. Your classmate must closely follow you and try to mirror your every move. After 30 to 60 seconds your classmate shouts "change." Immediately he or she becomes the leader and you become the follower. Continue the exercise for 5 to 10 minutes, switching roles every 30 to 60 seconds. Begin dribbling at half speed, then increase the pace to three-quarter speed by the end of the exercise.

COOL-DOWN

At the end of your training session it is a good idea to spend a few minutes allowing your heart rate and body functions to return to the resting state. During this time, often referred to as the *cool-down*, select a stretching exercise for each major muscle group that you used during the practice session. Include the hamstrings and quadriceps, calves, groin, and back. Postpractice stretching prevents next-day soreness. Remember, don't bounce or jerk when extending your muscles. Assume your stretch position, hold that position, then relax for a few seconds. Repeat each stretch twice.

Step 1 Passing and Receiving Ground Balls

Players use passing and receiving skills to play the ball from one teammate to another. These skills always occur in combination because each passed ball should be received and controlled by another player. Depending on the situation you may choose to either pass the ball along the ground or loft it through the air. As a general rule, pass the ball on the ground whenever possible. Rolling balls are relatively easier to receive and control than balls dropping from the air. Three ground passing techniques are commonly used—inside-of-the-foot, outside-of-the-foot, and instep passes. Again depending on the particular situation, two different receiving techniques are generally used to control ground passes—the inside-of-the-foot and outside-of-the-foot techniques.

WHY ARE PASSING AND RECEIVING GROUND BALLS IMPORTANT?

Successful team play depends in part on accurate passing as well as the ability to receive and control ground balls. Correct technique, pace or speed, and timing of release are critical elements in successful passing combinations. Just as important is the ability to receive and control the ball as it arrives from a teammate. Poor passing and receiving skills ultimately result in losing possession of the ball.

HOW TO EXECUTE THE INSIDE-OF-THE-FOOT PASS

Successful combination passing with your teammates requires that you consistently pass the ball with accuracy and correct pace. The inside-of-the-foot pass is the first skill you must master on your staircase to success. It is the most accurate method of passing the ball over distances of 15 yards or less. The technique is quite simple and involves little or no deception. Face your target as you approach the ball. Plant your nonkicking foot (e.g., balance foot) to the side of the ball. Contact the ball with the inside portion of your kicking foot and pass the ball in the direction you are facing. Make sure your kicking foot is firmly positioned as you follow through with the kicking motion (see Figure 1.1a-c).

HOW TO EXECUTE THE OUTSIDE-OF-THE-FOOT PASS

You will often have to pass the ball while moving at speed, and you may not want to pass the ball in the direction you are facing. For example, you must be able to pass the ball to a teammate positioned diagonally to your left or right. The outside-of-the-foot pass is your most appropriate choice in those situations. It is an excellent method for playing the ball diagonally to the right or left without breaking stride. The outside-of-the-foot pass also involves an element of deception and is less predictable to opponents than the inside-of-the-foot pass.

Use the outside-of-the-foot technique for short- and medium-distance passes. Stride forward and plant your balance foot slightly behind and to the side of the ball. Extend your kicking foot down and slightly inward, and contact the inside half of the ball with the outside portion of your instep. This kicking motion imparts spin to the ball because you strike it slightly off center. Use a complete follow-through of the kicking leg to give the pass distance and velocity (see Figure 1.1d-f).

HOW TO EXECUTE THE INSTEP PASS

The instep pass is your best choice to pass the ball over distances of 25 yards or more. The instep portion of your foot is covered by the laces of your shoe and provides a hard, flat surface with which to contact the ball. To execute the instep pass, approach the ball from a slight angle. Plant your nonkicking foot beside the ball with the balance leg flexed at the knee. Your nonkicking foot should be pointed in the general direction of the target. Extend your kicking foot down and keep it firmly positioned as you contact the center of the ball with your instep. Square your shoulders to the intended target at the instant you kick the ball. Keep your head down and focus your vision on the ball. Use a complete follow-through motion as you kick through the point of contact with the ball. Your kicking foot should rise to waist level or higher on the follow-through (see Figure 1.1g-i).

Figure 1.1 Keys to Success: Passing Ground Balls

Preparation Phase

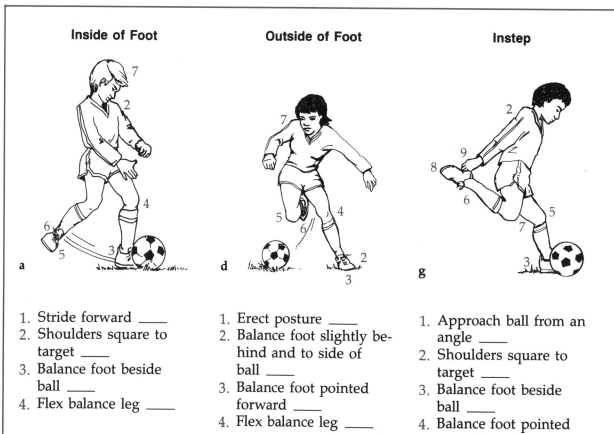

Inside of Foot

a

1. Stride forward ____
2. Shoulders square to target ____
3. Balance foot beside ball ____
4. Flex balance leg ____

Outside of Foot

d

1. Erect posture ____
2. Balance foot slightly behind and to side of ball ____
3. Balance foot pointed forward ____
4. Flex balance leg ____

Instep

g

1. Approach ball from an angle ____
2. Shoulders square to target ____
3. Balance foot beside ball ____
4. Balance foot pointed toward target ____

Inside of Foot	**Outside of Foot**	**Instep**
5. Turn kicking foot sideways ____	5. Swing kicking leg back ____	5. Flex balance leg ____
6. Swing kicking leg back ____	6. Kicking foot pointed down and rotated in ____	6. Kicking leg drawn back ____
7. Head down and steady ____	7. Focus vision on ball ____	7. Knee of kicking leg over ball ____
8. Focus vision on ball ____		8. Kicking foot extended and firm ____
		9. Arms to sides for balance ____
		10. Focus vision on ball ____

Execution Phase

Inside of Foot	**Outside of Foot**	**Instep**

b   e   h

Inside of Foot	**Outside of Foot**	**Instep**
1. Body over ball ____	1. Arms extended to sides for balance ____	1. Weight moves forward ____
2. Swing kicking leg forward ____	2. Snap kicking leg forward ____	2. Powerful forward motion of kicking leg ____
3. Kicking foot firm ____	3. Kicking foot firmly positioned ____	3. Contact center of ball ____
4. Use inside portion of foot ____	4. Head down and body over ball ____	4. Maintain firm position of kicking foot ____
5. Contact center of ball ____	5. Contact ball with outside of instep ____	
	6. Contact ball just inside its vertical midline ____	

Follow-Through
Phase

Inside of Foot	Outside of Foot	Instep

Inside of Foot

1. Transfer weight forward ____
2. Momentum through ball ____
3. Complete follow-through ____
4. Maintain position square to target ____

Outside of Foot

1. Transfer weight forward ____
2. Use an inside-out kicking motion ____
3. Complete follow-through of kicking leg ____

Instep

1. Momentum through ball ____
2. Weight centered over ball of balance foot ____
3. Follow through to chest level ____
4. Balance foot leaves ground ____
5. Land on ball of kicking foot ____

Detecting Ground Pass Errors

The most common errors players make when passing balls along the ground are listed here along with suggested methods to correct them. Most errors are due to incorrect passing technique.

ERROR 🚫   **CORRECTION**

Inside-of-the-Foot Pass

1. Your pass goes up in the air.

1. Contacting the ball too far forward on your foot can cause your foot to get under the ball, popping it in the air. Contact the center of the ball with the inside portion of your kicking foot between the ankle and the toes.

ERROR ⊘	CORRECTION
2. Your pass lacks accuracy.	2. Place your balance foot beside the ball with toes pointed toward your target. Square your shoulders to the target as you contact the ball.
3. Your pass lacks sufficient velocity or pace.	3. Keep your kicking foot firm and follow through with a smooth motion of the kicking leg.

Outside-of-the-Foot Pass

1. Your pass travels up in the air.	1. Plant your balance foot slightly behind and to the side of the ball. Lean forward as your foot contacts the ball. Keep your head down and focus your vision on the ball.
2. Your pass lacks sufficient power and pace.	2. Contact the ball with as much of your foot surface area as possible. Generate momentum through the ball with a complete follow-through motion of your kicking leg.
3. You impart too much spin to the ball and the pass lacks accuracy.	3. Contact the ball just left or right of its vertical midline, not on its outer edge.

Instep Pass

1. Your pass leaves the ground.	1. This occurs probably because you lean back as you kick the ball. Place your balance foot beside the ball, not behind it. Lean forward with the knee of your kicking leg over the ball as you kick it.
2. Your pass lacks accuracy.	2. Square your shoulders with the target as you contact the ball. Keep your kicking foot firm. Point your balance foot in the general direction of the intended target and pass the ball in the direction you are facing.
3. Your pass has too much spin on it.	3. Strike the ball directly through its center with the large area of your instep.

HOW TO RECEIVE A BALL WITH THE INSIDE OF THE FOOT

Align yourself with the oncoming ball. Point your balance foot toward the ball with the knee slightly flexed. Extend your receiving leg and foot toward the ball as it arrives. Keep your receiving foot firmly positioned with toes pointed up and away from the midline of your body. Cushion the impact of the ball by withdrawing your leg as the ball arrives. Don't stop the ball completely; rather, push it in the direction of your next movement (see Figure 1.2a-c).

HOW TO RECEIVE A BALL WITH THE OUTSIDE OF THE FOOT

At times you will have to receive and control a ball while you are tightly guarded (marked) by an opposing player. In that situation it is not appropriate to receive the ball with the inside of the foot because the opponent can reach in with his or her foot and kick the ball free. Instead, use the outside surface of your foot to receive a rolling ball. Position yourself sideways between your opponent and the oncoming ball. Use the foot farthest from the opponent to receive and control the ball. Rotate your receiving foot inward with toes pointing down toward the ground and contact the ball on the outside surface of your instep (see Figure 1.2d-f).

Figure 1.2 Keys to Success: Receiving Ground Balls

Preparation Phase

Inside of Foot

a

1. Align body with on-
   coming ball ____

Outside of Foot

d

1. Position sideways be-
   tween ball and
   opponent ____

Inside of Foot	**Outside of Foot**

Inside of Foot

2. Move toward ball ____
3. Position receiving foot sideways ____
4. Keep receiving foot firm ____
5. Extend receiving leg to meet ball ____
6. Focus vision on ball ____

Outside of Foot

2. Prepare to control ball with foot farthest from opponent ____
3. Extend receiving foot down and rotate inward ____
4. Keep receiving foot firm ____
5. Reach out receiving foot to meet ball ____
6. Focus vision on ball ____

**Execution
Phase**

Inside of Foot

b

1. Contact ball on inside of receiving foot ____
2. Withdraw receiving leg to cushion ball ____
3. Receive ball into space away from opponent ____

Outside of Foot

e

1. Control ball on outside of instep ____
2. Withdraw receiving leg and foot ____
3. Use body to shield ball from opponent ____
4. Turn ball into space away from opponent ____

**Follow-Through
Phase**

Inside of Foot

Outside of Foot

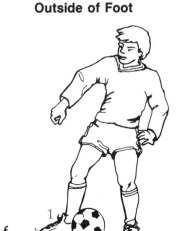

_____ 1. Push ball in direction of next movement _____

_____ 2. Head up with vision focused on field _____

Detecting Errors in Receiving Ground Balls

Although rolling balls are relatively easy to receive and control, you will make errors until you become familiar with the mechanics of the techniques. Common errors players make when receiving and controlling rolling balls are listed here.

ERROR ⊘

CORRECTION

Inside of the Foot

1. The ball rolls over your foot and out of your range of control.

2. The ball bounces away out of your range of control.

3. The ball rolls under your foot and out of your range of control.

1. Contact the center of the ball with the portion of your foot between the toes and the heel.

2. You must provide a ''soft target.'' Withdraw your receiving foot as the ball arrives to cushion the impact.

3. This error usually results from taking your eye off the ball. Focus your vision on the ball as it arrives.

ERROR   **CORRECTION**

Outside of the Foot

1. The ball bounces away out of your range of control.

2. The defender reaches in with his or her foot and kicks the ball away.

1. Withdraw your receiving foot to cushion the impact of the ball as it arrives.

2. Position your body sideways between the ball and your opponent. Control the ball with the foot farthest from the opponent.

Ground Ball Drills

1. Off the Wall

Position yourself with a ball approximately 5 yards from a wall or kickboard. Use the inside of the foot to pass the ball off the wall so it rebounds back to you. Receive and control each rebound with the inside of the foot, then pass it off the wall again. This is called two-touch passing—with the first touch you control the rolling ball, and with the second you pass it. Perform 40 inside-of-the-foot passes, alternately using your left and right feet to pass and receive.

Success Goal = 35 of 40 two-touch passes off the wall without error

Your Score = (#) _____ of 40 two-touch passes

2. Partner Pass

Face a classmate at a distance of approximately 5 yards. Kick a ball back and forth to each other using the inside-of-the-foot technique to pass and receive the ball. Alternate using your left and right feet to pass and receive the ball. Use two-touch passing. Concentrate on accuracy and proper pace of the pass.

Success Goal = 50 consecutive passes total (25 each) between you and your partner without error

Your Score = (#) _____ consecutive two-touch passes without error

3. Four-Wall Drill

Position yourself with a ball in the center of a racquetball court or small gymnasium. Pass the ball off a wall, receive and control the rebound, turn the ball into space toward an adjacent wall, pass the ball off that wall, receive the rebound and turn toward the third wall and pass, receive, and so on. Continue the circuit as you receive and control each pass that rebounds off the wall. Alternate passing the ball with the instep and the outside-of-the-foot techniques. Alternate receiving the ball with the inside and the outside of the foot. Attempt to pass and receive the ball off the wall using only two touches—one touch to pass and one to receive each rebounded ball. Execute a total of 48 passes (12 complete circuits around the court). Alternate feet when passing and receiving the ball for a total of 24 passes with each foot.

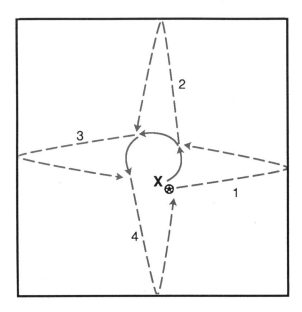

Success Goal = 40 of 48 passes received and controlled using two touches

Your Score = (#) _____ of 48 passes received and controlled

4. Partner to Partner

Position yourself 20 to 25 yards from a classmate. Use either the instep or the outside-of-the-foot technique to pass a stationary ball to your partner who controls and returns the ball in the same manner. Your partner should not have to move more than 2 yards in any direction to collect the ball. Alternate using your left and right feet to pass the ball. Receive the ball with either the inside or the outside of the foot. Use only two touches to receive and pass the ball. Perform 20 repetitions with each foot for a total of 40 balls received and passed to your partner.

Success Goals =

34 of 40 passes accurately passed within 2 yards right or left of your partner

36 of 40 balls received and returned to your partner using only two touches

Your Score =

(#) _____ of 40 passes within two yards of your partner

(#) _____ of 40 passes received and returned using only two touches

5. Receive, Pass, and Change Lines

Perform this drill with several classmates. Divide the group into two opposing lines of equal numbers approximately 10 yards apart. The first player in line 1 passes the ball to the first player in line 2 and then runs to the end of line 2. The player receiving the ball in line 2 controls it using the inside- or the outside-of-the-foot technique, then uses the inside of the foot to pass it to the next player in line 1. He or she then sprints to the end of line 1. Continue the drill until each player has passed and received 30 balls. Use only two touches to receive and pass the ball.

Success Goals =

   28 of 30 passes accurately played to a classmate in the opposite line

   28 of 30 passes received and returned using only two touches

Your Score =

   (#) _____ of 30 accurate passes

   (#) _____ of 30 balls received and returned using only two touches

6. Monkey in the Middle

Stand midway between two classmates positioned 20 yards apart; each of them has a ball. One classmate passes his or her ball to you. Move to the ball, receive it using the inside or the outside of the foot, and return it by using either an inside- or an outside-of-the-foot pass. Immediately turn and move toward the other classmate who passes his or her ball to you. Receive and return the ball using either the inside or the outside of the foot. Perform the exercise at maximum speed. Use only two touches to receive and pass the ball.

Success Goal = 18 of 20 passes received and returned without error using two touches to receive and pass the ball

Your Score = (#) _____ passes received and returned without error using two touches

7. *Pass and Follow*

Position yourself with a classmate 20 yards from a third player. Begin the exercise by passing a ball to the player 20 yards away. Immediately after your pass sprint to the position of the player receiving the ball. The player receiving the ball then passes it to the third player (in your original position) and sprints to that position. Emphasize the concept of passing the ball and then immediately sprinting to follow (i.e., support) your pass. Use either the outside-of-the-foot or the instep pass, and receive the ball with either the inside or the outside of the foot. Continue the exercise until each player has passed and received a total of 30 balls. Use only two touches to receive and pass the ball.

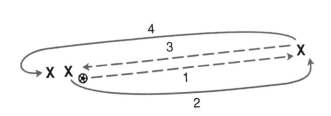

Success Goal = 25 of 30 balls received and accurately passed using only two touches

Your Score = (#) _____ of 30 balls received and accurately passed using only two touches

8. *Pass and Receive With a Moving Target*

Play with two classmates in an area approximately 40 yards square. Begin the exercise with a ball; your classmates are positioned at least 25 yards from you. On your command your classmates begin moving in random fashion within the designated area. Pass the ball to either of them using an instep or an outside-of-the-foot pass. Immediately sprint to a position near the player with the ball, receive a short return pass, and then pass the ball to the third player as he or she continues to move within the area. All players should be moving constantly during the entire drill. Use only two touches to receive and pass the ball. All your passes should be 25 yards or longer. Execute 20 passes, then switch roles with one of your teammates.

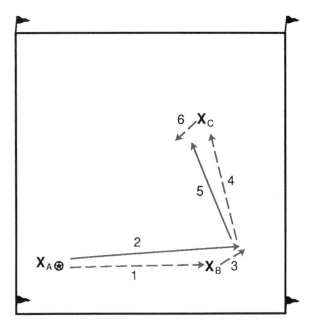

Success Goal = 16 of 20 balls received and accurately passed to classmates using only two touches

Your Score = (#) _____ of 20 balls received and accurately passed using two touches

9. Circle Drill

Select three classmates to participate in this exercise with you. Position yourselves evenly around a circle with a diameter of 24 to 30 yards. Number yourselves 1, 2, 3, and 4. You are number 1; begin the exercise with possession of the ball. Pass it to player number 2 and sprint to his or her position on the circle. Player 2 receives the ball, controls it, passes it to player number 3, and sprints to that spot. Player 3 passes to player 4 and does the same. The passing cycle is completed with player 4 passing to player 1. You can pass and receive the ball using any of the techniques discussed in this step. Continue the drill until each player has passed and received 40 balls. Use only two touches; control the ball with your first touch and pass to a classmate with the second.

Success Goal = 35 of 40 balls received and passed using only two touches

Your Score = (#) _____ of 40 balls received and passed using only two touches

10. Keep-Away

Work with three other players in this drill. Use cones or flags to mark off a grid area approximately 10 yards square. Two players and you form the attacking team and attempt to keep the ball away from the fourth player (defender) within the grid. Use any of the passing and receiving techniques that are appropriate in this situation. The defender tries to steal the ball by pressuring the player who has the ball. The attacking team scores 1 point each time it makes 10 consecutive passes without interception by the defender. This exercise is more difficult than the previous drills because it incorporates the game-related pressures of restricted space, player movement, and a defending opponent. Play the game for 5 minutes, then rearrange players and repeat. Each player should have a turn as the defender.

Success Goal = attacking team scores a minimum of 5 points in a 5-minute game

Your Score = (#) _____ of points scored as the attacking team in a 5-minute game

Passing and Receiving Ground Balls Keys to Success Checklists

Someone observing your passing and receiving skills should focus on specific aspects of your performance as well as your overall motion. You must be able to execute all passing and receiving skills in a comfortable, relaxed manner; you shouldn't look stiff or robot-like. Ask a trained observer—your teacher, your coach, or a knowledgeable classmate—to observe your inside-of-the-foot, outside-of-the-foot, and instep pass techniques and your inside-of-the-foot and outside-of-the-foot pass reception techniques. The observer can use the checklists in Figures 1.1 and 1.2 to evaluate your performance and provide corrective feedback.

Step 2 Passing and Receiving Lofted Balls

Now that you are familiar with the methods of passing and receiving ground balls, you will progress to passing and receiving lofted, or chipped, balls. Two basic techniques, the *short chip* and the *long chip*, are used to loft a pass. Which pass you use depends on the distance the ball must travel. You can use various body surfaces, including your instep, thighs, chest, and head, to receive and control balls that drop from the air. Your choice of body surface will depend on the ball's flight trajectory and whether you are being pressured by an opponent.

WHY ARE PASSING AND RECEIVING LOFTED BALLS IMPORTANT?

Usually it is best to pass the ball along the ground rather than through the air because it is easier for teammates to receive and control a rolling ball. Even so, in certain game situations a lofted pass will be your best alternative. For example, a defending player may be blocking the passing lane to a teammate who is open and in a dangerous attacking position. Or you may decide to loft a pass into the space behind the opposing defense for a swift-running teammate. A lofted ball can even be used to score a goal if the opposing goalkeeper drifts too far forward of the goal line. To take advantage of those special situations you must become adept at chipping the ball over varying distances.

It is also important that you develop the ability to receive and control lofted balls. The ball frequently leaves the ground during a soccer match. Chip passes, goal kicks, crossed balls, corner kicks, and defensive clearances are usually received directly out of the air. You will enhance your opportunities for individual and team success if you master the skills used to receive and control lofted balls.

HOW TO EXECUTE THE SHORT CHIP PASS

The short chip pass is commonly used when a passing lane is blocked by a defending opponent. This can occur during the normal course of action or on a free kick when the defending team has formed a wall of players to block your shot. The short chip pass is particularly effective in such situations because it enables you to exploit the space behind defending players.

Approach the ball from a slight angle. Place your balance foot directly beside the ball, draw back your kicking leg, and extend your kicking foot. Square your shoulders with the target and keep your kicking foot firmly positioned as you drive it underneath the ball. Use a short, powerful snap motion of your kicking leg. It is important that you wedge your instep underneath the ball, because the pass must achieve sufficient height to clear an opponent standing only a few yards from you. Only minimal follow-through motion is required for passes of 10 to 15 yards. Try to impart a slight backspin on the ball as you kick it. Backspin makes for a softer pass that is easy for a teammate to control. Backspin normally results when your foot contacts the lower portion of the ball (see Figure 2.1a-c).

HOW TO EXECUTE THE LONG CHIP PASS

The kicking mechanics used for the long chip pass are somewhat similar to those used for the short chip pass. Approach the ball from a slight angle. Place your balance foot to the side of and slightly behind the ball. The position of your balance foot differs slightly from that used for the short chip pass. Planting your foot behind the ball allows for the greater follow-through motion of your kicking leg necessary to propel the ball over longer distances. As with the short chip pass, extend your kicking foot, keep it firm, and drive the instep through the lower half of the ball. Lean back as you contact the ball (see Figure 2.1d-f).

Figure 2.1 Keys to Success: *Chip Passes*

Preparation Phase

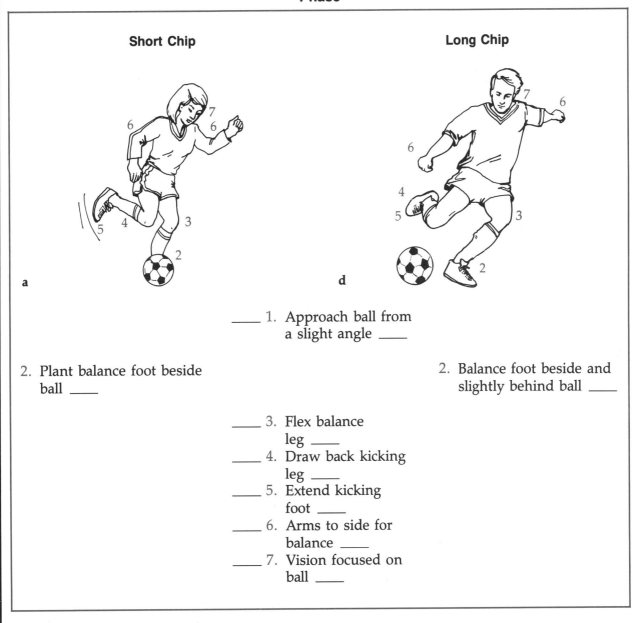

Short Chip

Long Chip

a

d

_____ 1. Approach ball from a slight angle _____

2. Plant balance foot beside ball _____

2. Balance foot beside and slightly behind ball _____

_____ 3. Flex balance leg _____
_____ 4. Draw back kicking leg _____
_____ 5. Extend kicking foot _____
_____ 6. Arms to side for balance _____
_____ 7. Vision focused on ball _____

Execution
Phase

Short Chip   **Long Chip**

b   e

_____ 1. Knee of kicking leg over ball _____

2. Lean slightly forward _____

_____ 3. Square shoulders with target _____

_____ 4. Drive instep of kicking foot under ball _____

_____ 5. Kicking foot firm _____

2. Lean slightly backward _____

6. Short, powerful kicking motion _____
7. Arms swing forward _____
8. Impart backspin to ball _____

6. Arms move forward _____
7. Impart backspin to ball _____

**Follow-Through
Phase**

Short Chip

c

1. Weight moves forward over ball of balance foot ____
2. Kicking leg snaps straight ____
3. Minimal follow-through ____

Long Chip

f

1. Kicking leg snaps straight ____
2. Weight moves forward over ball of balance foot ____
3. Complete follow-through of kicking leg to waist level ____

Detecting Chip Pass Errors

Most errors that occur with chip passes can be attributed to improper position of either the kicking foot or the balance foot. Beginning players may also hesitate to wedge their foot under the ball for fear they will injure themselves. Most of these errors are easily corrected. Common chip pass errors are listed here along with suggestions for correcting them.

ERROR   **CORRECTION**

Short Chip Pass

1. Your pass has a low trajectory rather than a lofted trajectory.

1. Contact the bottom edge of the ball with the instep of your kicking foot. Use a short, powerful kicking motion as you drive your foot underneath the ball.

2. Your pass lacks accuracy.

2. Square your shoulders with the target as you kick the ball. Contact the ball with as much surface area of your instep as possible. Be sure to keep your kicking foot firmly positioned throughout the kicking motion.

Long Chip Pass

1. The ball fails to reach sufficient height to clear defending players.

1. Plant your balance foot to the side of and slightly behind the ball. Lean back and extend your foot as you contact the ball.

2. You do not generate sufficient distance on your pass.

2. Extend and firmly position your kicking foot as you drive your instep through the lower half of the ball. Use a full follow-through motion of your kicking leg.

3. Your pass lacks accuracy.

3. Square your shoulders with the intended target as you prepare to kick the ball. Contact the central area of the lower half of the ball. Make sure your kicking foot remains firm throughout the kicking motion.

HOW TO RECEIVE A LOFTED BALL WITH YOUR INSTEP

The instep portion of your foot provides an excellent surface with which to receive and control a ball from the air. This method of controlling the ball is best used when you are not under immediate pressure from a defending opponent. It is a basic technique that you can master with a little practice.

Imagine that your shoe is a glove and that you are going to catch the ball on the instep of your foot. First you must get in the proper position. Anticipate where the ball will drop, move to that spot, and then square your shoulders to the oncoming ball. Raise your receiving foot 12 to 18 inches off the ground to meet the ball as it descends. Extend your receiving foot parallel to the ground and keep it firmly positioned. Drop your foot to the ground as the ball contacts your instep. The downward movement of your receiving foot will cushion the impact and drop the ball at your feet (see Figure 2.2).

HOW TO RECEIVE A LOFTED BALL WITH YOUR THIGH

Sometimes you will not be in position to control a lofted ball with your instep due to the ball's trajectory of flight or the position of nearby opponents. The mid-thigh area of your upper leg is an alternative body surface you can use to receive and control the ball.

Anticipate the flight of the ball and move to the proper receiving position. Always position yourself between the ball and a defending opponent. Raise your receiving leg as the ball descends so that your thigh is parallel to the ground. Raise your arms to the sides and flex your balance leg slightly. Proper distribution of your body weight is essential for successful execution of this technique. Receive the ball on the middle part of your thigh. Imagine that your leg is on a hinge—at the instant the ball contacts your thigh withdraw your leg downward so that the ball drops softly at your feet (see Figure 2.3).

HOW TO RECEIVE A LOFTED BALL WITH YOUR CHEST

Your chest provides an excellent body surface with which you can receive and control a ball that drops from above. It is particularly effective when you are closely guarded by an opponent, because you can shield the ball with your body as you control it.

In preparing to receive you must move to a position in line with the oncoming ball. Arch your upper body backward and receive the ball on the upper central area of your chest. Although women are generally permitted to cross their arms against their chests and receive the ball on their arms, most high school and college women soccer players use the same receiving technique as men. Withdraw your upper body as the ball contacts your chest to cushion the impact. If you are tightly marked, control the ball into the space away from the opponent by turning your upper body in the direction you wish to move with the ball at the instant it contacts your chest (see Figure 2.4).

HOW TO RECEIVE A LOFTED BALL WITH YOUR HEAD

In most instances you use your head to pass the ball to a teammate, shoot on goal, or clear an air ball out of your defending zone. In some situations, however, you can use your head to receive and control a ball that drops from above. This is a difficult skill to successfully execute because it requires correct technique as well as precise timing.

In preparing to receive you should move to a position under the descending ball. Use a two-footed takeoff to jump up, and contact the ball at the highest point of your jump. Watch the ball, angle your head back, and contact the ball on the flat surface of your forehead. The timing of your jump is critical for success. Jump early to meet the ball. Your body should begin its descent to the ground at the instant the ball contacts your forehead. In this way you will provide a soft receiving surface. The ball should bounce slightly upward off your forehead and then drop to your feet (see Figure 2.5).

Figure 2.2 Keys to Success:
Receiving
a Lofted Ball
With Your Instep

**Preparation
Phase**

1. Move to receiving position ___
2. Align body with ball ___
3. Square shoulders with flight of ball ___
4. Raise receiving foot 12 to 18 inches from ground ___
5. Extend receiving foot and keep it firm ___
6. Flex balance leg ___
7. Arms to side for balance ___
8. Focus vision on ball ___

a

**Execution
Phase**

1. Receive ball on instep ___
2. Withdraw receiving foot to ground ___
3. Drop ball within range of control ___

b

**Follow-Through
Phase**

1. Push ball into open
   space ___

2. Head up with vision
   focused on field ___

Figure 2.3 Keys to Success:
**Receiving
a Lofted Ball
With Your Thigh**

**Preparation
Phase**

1. Position body under
   descending ball ___
2. Raise receiving leg ___
3. Thigh parallel to
   ground ___
4. Arms out to sides for
   balance ___
5. Slightly flex balance
   leg ___
6. Focus vision on ball ___

a

**Execution
Phase**

1. Receive ball on mid-
   thigh ___
2. Withdraw thigh
   downward ___
3. Collect ball at feet ___
4. Shield ball from
   opponent ___

b

**Follow-Through
Phase**

1. Push ball to open
   space ____
2. Head up with vision
   focused on field ____

c

Figure 2.4 Keys to Success:
**Receiving a
Lofted Ball
With Your Chest**

**Preparation
Phase**

1. Align body with on-
   coming ball ____
2. Face ball with shoulders
   square ____
3. Arch upper body
   back ____
4. Bend knees slightly ____
5. Arms out to sides for
   balance ____
6. Focus vision on ball ____

a

Execution
Phase

1. Receive ball on upper chest area ____
2. Withdraw chest to cushion impact ____
3. Turn upper body as ball arrives ____
4. Control ball into space away from opponent ____

b

Follow-Through
Phase

1. Shield ball from opponent ____
2. Push ball in direction of next movement ____
3. Head up with vision focused on field ____

c

Figure 2.5 Keys to Success:
Receiving a
Lofted Ball
With Your Head

**Preparation
Phase**

1. Position body under
   descending ball ____
2. Flex knees slightly ____
3. Arms extended back and
   to sides ____
4. Head steady with vision
   focused on ball ____

a

**Execution
Phase**

1. Jump early as ball
   descends ____
2. Use two-footed
   takeoff ____
3. Arch upper body ____
4. Eyes open ____
5. Angle forehead
   back ____
6. Meet ball at highest
   point of jump ____
7. Contact ball on
   forehead ____
8. Withdraw head on
   contact ____

b

**Follow-Through
Phase**

1. Land on both feet ____
2. Drop ball to feet ____
3. Head up with vision focused on field ____
4. Push ball into open space ____

c

Detecting Errors in Receiving Lofted Balls

Receiving and controlling a ball that drops from above requires confidence as well as proper technique. Always try to present a soft, relaxed surface as you receive the ball. You may tend to be stiff or rigid if you are unsure of yourself, which will undoubtedly lead to performance errors. As you become ac- customed to the various methods of receiving lofted balls you will gain confidence and become more relaxed. It is not uncommon for beginners to experience difficulty, however. The following material discusses common performance errors and suggestions to correct them.

ERROR

CORRECTION

Receiving a Lofted Ball With Your Instep

1. The ball bounces up out of control after contacting your instep.

1. Early preparation is essential. Raise your receiving foot to meet the ball as it descends. Withdraw your foot downward at the instant the ball contacts your instep. Remember to always provide a soft target to cushion the impact of the ball.

ERROR ⊘	CORRECTION
2. The ball bounces forward after contacting your instep.	2. You may lose control if you receive the ball too far forward on your foot, near the toes. Remember to keep your foot firmly positioned as you receive the ball on the central area of your instep.
3. The ball spins back into your body instead of dropping to the ground at your feet.	3. This error occurs because your receiving foot is pointed up rather than fully extended. Extend your receiving foot so it is approximately parallel to the ground as the ball contacts the instep.

Receiving a Lofted Ball With Your Thigh

1. The ball bounces up out of control on contact with your thigh.	1. This occurs because your leg is moving up as the ball contacts your thigh. Raise your thigh into the receiving position before the ball arrives. Withdraw your thigh downward as the ball contacts your leg.
2. The ball bounces forward off your thigh.	2. This usually occurs because you receive the ball too far forward on your thigh, near the kneecap. Receive the ball on the central area of your thigh, which provides a large, soft surface. The muscle tissue of the mid-thigh area aids in cushioning the impact of the ball.

Receiving a Lofted Ball With Your Chest

1. The ball bounces forward off your chest and out of your range of control.	1. Receive the ball just to the right or left of center chest, where muscle and soft tissue provide an excellent receiving surface. Withdraw your upper body back a few inches as the ball contacts your chest.
2. The ball bounces up off your chest.	2. This occurs because you arch your upper body too far back. Arch back only a few inches from the vertical position as you receive the ball.

ERROR   **CORRECTION**

**Receiving a Lofted Ball
With Your Head**

1. The ball bounces up and out of control off your forehead.

2. The ball glances sideways off your head.

1. You jumped too late and as a result are still moving upward as the ball contacts your forehead. Leave the ground early so that your body is beginning to descend as the ball arrives.

2. Always receive the ball on the large, flat surface of your forehead, not the side or top of your head. Keep your vision focused on the ball until it contacts your head.

Lofted Ball Drills

1. Short Chip to Chest

Face a partner at a distance of 3 to 4 yards. Use a short, powerful kicking motion to chip a stationary ball to your partner's chest. Your partner controls the ball on his or her chest, drops it to the ground, and then returns it to you. Execute 25 chip passes with each foot, then change roles with your partner.

Success Goals =

40 of 50 passes chipped to partner's chest (partner not permitted to move more than one step in either direction to control the ball)

45 of 50 chipped balls received and controlled with chest and dropped to feet

Your Score =

(#) _____ of 50 passes chipped to partner's chest

(#) _____ of 50 chipped balls received and controlled with chest and dropped to feet

2. Chip Over Goal

Position yourself with a ball 10 yards in front of a regulation goal. A classmate is positioned at an equal distance from the goal on the opposite side. Attempt to chip a stationary ball over the crossbar (which is 8 feet high) to your classmate who controls the ball and returns it to you in the same manner. It is essential that your pass quickly achieve sufficient height to clear the goal. Execute 40 repetitions, 20 with each foot. Award yourself 1 point for each chip pass that clears the crossbar and drops to the ground within 3 feet of your classmate. Your classmate receives the ball using either the instep or thigh and is awarded 1 point for each ball controlled and dropped to the ground. Your classmate then returns the ball by chipping it over the goal. You receive and control the ball in the same manner.

Success Goals =

30 of 40 possible points passing

35 of 40 possible points receiving

Your Score =

(#) _____ of 40 possible points passing

(#) _____ of 40 possible points receiving

3. Grid-to-Grid Chip

Use cones or flags to mark off two 10-by-10-yard grids approximately 25 yards apart. Position yourself with a ball in one grid while a classmate is positioned in the other. Attempt to chip a stationary ball back and forth to each other. Receive the ball using the instep, thigh, chest, or head. Scoring occurs as follows. You are awarded 2 points for each chip pass that drops directly out of the air within your classmate's grid; if your pass bounces into the grid on one hop you receive 1 point. You also score 1 point for each lofted ball you receive, control, and return using three or fewer touches. Execute 50 chip passes, 25 with each foot.

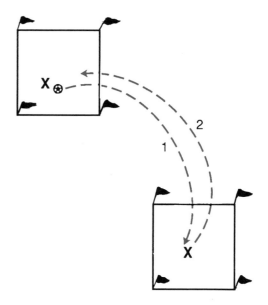

Success Goals =

70 of a possible 100 points passing

45 of 50 possible points receiving

Your Score =

(#) ____ of 100 possible points passing

(#) ____ of 50 possible points receiving

4. Pass and Receive in Threes

Select two classmates to participate with you in this exercise. Position yourself midway between the classmates who are standing 25 yards apart. Each classmate has a ball at his or her feet. One classmate chips a ball to you. Receive and control the ball out of the air using the appropriate body surface, then return it to the server by passing it along the ground. Immediately turn toward the other classmate and receive a lofted ball from him or her. Continue the exercise, receiving a lofted ball from one classmate and then the other. Receive 15 lofted passes from each server, then switch places with one of the servers. Continue until all players have passed and received 30 lofted balls.

Success Goals =

25 of 30 passes chipped to the receiver so that he or she can receive the ball out of the air

25 of 30 lofted balls received and controlled at feet using only two touches

Your Score =

(#) ____ of 30 passes accurately chipped to the receiver

(#) ____ of 30 passes received and controlled using only two touches

5. Chip a Rolling Ball

Select two classmates to participate with you in this exercise. Face one of your classmates at a distance of 25 yards with the third player positioned with a ball midway between you. The player in the center serves a rolling ball to you. Attempt to chip the rolling ball over the server's head to the classmate standing 25 yards away. The player receiving the lofted pass can receive and control the ball using any of the techniques discussed earlier. All players rotate positions after each pass—the classmate who served you the ball moves to your original position, the classmate who received your chip pass moves to the middle, and you follow your pass as you move to the opposite end of the line. Repeat the drill and rotate positions again. Continue the exercise until each player has chipped and received 40 passes. Alternate feet when chipping the ball. Do not get discouraged if you initially experience difficulty executing this drill. Accurately chipping a rolling ball is a difficult skill to master and requires much practice.

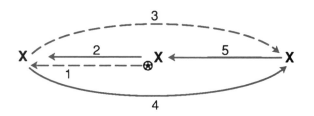

Success Goals =

20 of 40 passes accurately chipped over the server to within 5 feet of the classmate positioned 25 yards away

30 of 40 lofted balls received and controlled within a 3-foot radius of your feet

Your Score =

(#) _____ of 40 accurate passes

(#) _____ of 40 lofted balls successfully received and controlled

6. Two-Person Team Tennis

Play this game on a tennis or volleyball court. Team up with a classmate on one side of the net with your opponents positioned on the opposite side. Flip a coin to determine which team serves first. To serve you must chip the ball over the net. The receiving team can control the ball directly out of the air or after it bounces once. If the ball bounces two or more times in the opponent's court, or if the receiving team fails to return the serve over the net, the serving team is awarded 1 point and retains service. The player receiving the ball is permitted one touch to control it and a second touch to play it over the net or to his or her teammate.

Teammates are permitted to pass the ball to each other in the air before returning it over the net. Once the ball has been received, however, it must be returned over the net before it drops to the ground. Change of serve occurs if the ball is served out of the playing court or if the serving team fails to properly receive the return of service. Only the serving team can score points. The first team to score 15 points wins the game. Play a best-of-five-games match.

Success Goal = your team scores 15 points before your opponents score 15 points

Your Score =

(#) _____ your team's points

(#) _____ opponents' points

7. Numbers Passing Game

Select three classmates to participate in this exercise with you. Each player calls out a number, beginning with you as number 1 and continuing up through the number of players (4). You begin with possession of the ball. All players begin jogging in random fashion within a field area of 40 by 50 yards. Chip the ball to player 2 who receives the ball and passes to player 3, who likewise receives and passes the ball to player 4. Player 4 completes the cycle by passing back to you. All players remain in constant motion throughout the exercise, whether they possess the ball or not. Use long or short chip passes; receive and control the ball out of the air with the appropriate body surface. Continue the exercise until each player has received and controlled 25 lofted balls. An accurate chip pass is one that a classmate can receive directly out of the air. Successful control is a lofted ball that is received and controlled using only two touches.

Success Goals =

20 of 25 lofted passes accurately served to a moving classmate

20 of 25 lofted balls successfully received and controlled

Your Score =

(#) _____ of 25 accurately lofted passes

(#) _____ of 25 lofted balls successfully received and controlled

Passing and Receiving Lofted Balls
Keys to Success Checklists

Ask a trained observer—your teacher, your coach, or a knowledgeable classmate—to observe your skill at chipping passes over both short and long distances and receiving lofted balls. The observer can use the checklists in Figures 2.1, 2.2, 2.3, 2.4, and 2.5 to evaluate your overall performance and provide corrective feedback.

Step 3 Individual Ball Possession

Soccer players use the individual ball possession skills of *dribbling* and *shielding* in combination to move while maintaining possession of the ball. Dribbling in soccer serves the same basic function as dribbling in basketball—it enables a player to possess the ball while running past opponents or into open space. You can use various surfaces of your foot (inside, outside, instep, sole) to contact the ball while dribbling. Unlike in most other soccer skills, however, there is not just one correct method of dribbling. You can develop your own style as long as you achieve the primary objective of beating an opponent while maintaining possession of the ball.

You must remember, however, that excessive dribbling serves no useful purpose. In fact, it can destroy the vital teamwork needed for successful attacking soccer. As a general rule, refrain from taking on opponents in the defending third of the field nearest your own goal. Losing ball possession in that area could result in an opponent's score. Dribbling skills can be used to best advantage in the attacking third of the field near the opponent's goal. If you successfully take on (i.e., dribble at) and beat a defender in that area you've created an opportunity to score. Two basic types of dribbling skills are used in game competition—dribbling for close control in a crowd of players, and dribbling for speed in open space. Players often use shielding skills in conjunction with dribbling skills to protect the ball from an opponent trying to gain possession.

WHY ARE DRIBBLING AND SHIELDING SKILLS IMPORTANT?

Successful attacking play depends in part on each player's ability to maintain possession of the ball when challenged by defending opponents. The ability to beat your opponent in a one-versus-one situation is essential to individual as well as team success. Dribbling skills can be used at opportune times to take on defending players and create scoring opportunities for yourself and teammates.

The soccer ball is a very precious commodity. It must be shared by 22 players during the course of a match. When you have possession of the ball you can be quite sure that opponents will attempt to steal it from you. It is essential that you develop the skills you need to maintain possession of the ball. You can protect the ball from a challenging opponent by shielding it with your body.

HOW TO DRIBBLE FOR CLOSE CONTROL

Dribbling is an art created by the individual in possession of the ball. Each player develops his or her own dribbling identity or personality. Regardless of individual differences, however, all successful dribbling styles have several common elements. These include sudden changes of speed and direction, body feints, deceptive movements, and close control of the ball. Whatever your dribbling style, be sure to incorporate these elements into your technique.

When dribbling in a crowd of opposing players you must keep close control of the ball so you don't lose possession. Imagine that the ball is tied to your toes by a short string. It should never go farther than the length of the string from your feet. Quick changes of speed and direction will unbalance opponents and create additional space in which to dribble and maneuver with the ball (see Figure 3.1a-c).

HOW TO DRIBBLE FOR SPEED

You will not always have to dribble for close control. At times you will receive and possess the ball in open space. For example, you may receive a pass in the space between the opposing team's midfielders and defenders. Or you may find yourself with the ball behind the opponent's defense in a breakaway situation. To take best advantage of such situations you must be able to run at speed while dribbling the ball. Doing so requires a different dribbling technique than that used for close control. Push the ball several feet ahead of you into open space, sprint to it, and then push it again. Use the outside surface of your instep to push the ball forward (see Figure 3.1d-f).

Figure 3.1 Keys to Success: *Dribbling*

Preparation Phase

For Close Control

a

1. Knees flexed ____
2. Crouched position ____
3. Low center of gravity ____
4. Body over ball ____
5. Head up when possible ____

For Speed

d

1. Upright posture ____
2. Ball at your feet ____
3. Head up for good field vision ____

Execution
Phase

For Close Control

b

1. Focus vision on ball ____
2. Use body feints ____
3. Push ball with appropriate surface of foot ____
4. Change speed, direction, or both ____

For Speed

e

1. Head down with vision on ball ____
2. Contact ball with instep or outside of foot ____
3. Push ball ahead several feet ____

Follow-Through
Phase

For Close Control

c

1. Maintain close control ____

For Speed

f

1. Head up for good field vision ____

For Close Control	**For Speed**
2. Accelerate away from opponent ____	2. Sprint to ball ____
3. Look up with vision focused on field ____	3. Push ball again ____

Detecting Errors in Dribbling

Because the techniques used in dribbling for close control differ from those used when dribbling for speed, performance errors also differ. Even slight errors in judgment or technique can result in loss of possession when you are dribbling in a crowd of players. When you are dribbling in open space the margin for error is not so precise. Common dribbling errors are listed here along with suggestions for correcting them.

ERROR

CORRECTION

Dribbling for Close Control

1. The ball rolls too far from your feet, out of your control.

2. The ball gets tangled between your feet when you dribble.

Dribbling for Speed

1. You feel awkward when pushing the ball forward into open space.

1. Try to keep the ball under your body, as close to your feet as possible. In that position you can change direction quickly and the ball is always within your immediate control. Develop a soft touch, nudging the ball gently with your foot as you dribble.

2. Don't try to be too fancy or attempt too many body movements when taking on an opponent. Become comfortable and proficient with a few different dribbling moves and use those to beat opponents.

1. The most comfortable method of pushing the ball forward when dribbling at speed is using the outside surface of the instep. Extend your kicking foot down and inward as you contact the ball. Do not use the inside surface of your foot to push the ball because you cannot maintain a smooth, comfortable running motion with that technique.

ERROR   **CORRECTION**

2. You have difficulty running at speed while dribbling the ball.

2. Remember to push the ball several feet ahead of you and then sprint to it. Do not touch the ball every step or two as you would when dribbling for close control.

HOW TO SHIELD THE BALL

Correct placement of your body in relation to the ball and your opponent is very important. Position yourself sideways between the ball and the challenging opponent. Assume a slightly crouched position and control the ball with the foot farthest from the opponent. In the crouched position you have a wide base of support and can create greater distance between the opponent and the ball. Use body feints and deceptive movements to unbalance the challenging player. Remember that the ball must always be within your range of control when you are shielding an opponent. If not, the referee can penalize you for unfairly obstructing the opponent from the ball (see Figure 3.2).

Figure 3.2 *Keys to Success: Shielding the Ball*

Preparation Phase

1. Keep close control of ball ____
2. Crouched stance ____
3. Position sideways to opponent ____
4. Arms out to sides for balance ____
5. Head up with vision focused on opponent ____

a

**Execution
Phase**

1. Control ball with foot farthest from opponent ____
2. Control ball with outside, inside, or sole of foot ____
3. Maintain wide base of support ____
4. Alternate vision from ball to opponent ____
5. Use body feints to unbalance opponent ____
6. Use quick changes of direction ____

b

**Follow-Through
Phase**

1. Readjust body position in response to opponent ____

2. Maintain crouched position ____
3. Maintain space between ball and opponent ____

Detecting Errors in Shielding the Ball

Most errors result from incorrect positioning of the body in relation to the ball and the opponent. You must constantly readjust your position in response to the movements of the challenging player. To do that you must feel the pressure of the opponent and move the ball away from the pressure. Common errors players make when shielding the ball are discussed here along with suggested methods of correcting them.

ERROR ⃠	CORRECTION
1. The challenging player reaches in with his or her foot and dislodges the ball from your possession.	1. Position your body sideways to the defender in a slightly crouched position. Your feet should be approximately shoulder-width apart. Control the ball with the foot farthest from the opponent. Always maintain as much space as possible between the ball and your opponent.
2. You have poor balance and are easily knocked off the ball by a legal shoulder charge from the challenging player.	2. Poor balance usually results from standing erect with your feet too close together. Maintain the crouched stance with feet apart. In this position your weight is centered and you have the greatest stability.

Dribbling and Shielding Drills

1. Individual Dribble

Dribble in random fashion within a large field area. Use various surfaces of your foot (inside, outside, instep, sole) to contact the ball. Combine changes of direction and speed into your dribbling pattern. For example, cut the ball with the instep of your right foot to change direction, then accelerate into space by pushing the ball ahead with the outside of your left foot. Imagine that there are opposing players all around you, so emphasize close control of the ball. Dribble continuously until you have touched the ball 150 times with various surfaces of your feet.

Success Goal = 150 touches of the ball without loss of control

Your Score = (#) _____ touches without loss of control

2. Shadow Dribbling

This exercise is similar to the previous drill except that a classmate must try to closely follow, or shadow, you as you dribble a ball within the field area. Your objective is to "lose" your shadow through a series of changes of speed and direction. You are awarded 1 point each time you lose your shadow—that is, get a distance of 3 yards between yourself and your classmate. Keep the ball under close control at all times. Shield the ball with your body if the shadow gets too close. Dribble continuously for a period of 4 minutes, then switch roles with your classmate.

Success Goal = 15 points in 4 minutes of dribbling

Your Score = (#) _____ points

3. Slalom Dribble

Set up a line of five cones spaced 2 yards apart. Imagine that the cones are opposing players. Begin at the first cone and dribble in and out of the cones until you get to the last one, then turn and dribble in and out of the cones back to the starting line. Keep the ball under close control at all times. Repeat the slalom dribble circuit 20 times with a short rest period between repetitions. Knocking down a cone is considered a dribbling error. Award yourself 1 point for each complete circuit through the cones without error.

Success Goal = 18 of a possible 20 points

Your Score = (#) _____ points

4. Cone to Cone

Select a classmate to participate with you in this exercise. Position two cones approximately 10 yards apart along a line. Stand on one side of the line midway between the cones with a ball while your classmate faces you without a ball on the other side. Neither of you is allowed to cross the line. Your objective is to dribble the ball laterally to one cone or the other before your classmate can get there. Use body feints, deceptive movements, and changes of speed and direction. Your classmate tries to react to your every move so you can't beat him or her to a cone with the ball. You are awarded 1 point for each time you dribble and stop the ball at a cone before your classmate can establish position there. Play the game for 2 minutes, rest, then switch roles with your classmate and play again.

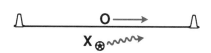

Success Goal = 5 points scored in 2-minute game

Your Score = (#) ___ points

5. Soccer Marbles

Select two classmates to participate with you in this exercise. Play in an area approximately 25 by 25 yards. Each player has a ball. You are designated as "it" to begin the game. Dribble anywhere within the area while your classmates dribble after you and try to contact your ball with their own. Each time a classmate hits your ball with his or hers counts as 1 penalty point against you. Play the game for 3 minutes, then switch roles with one of your classmates. Use quick changes of speed and direction and shielding skills to prevent classmates from hitting your ball.

Success Goal = less than 5 penalty points in 3 minutes

Your Score = (#) ___ penalty points

6. *Speed Dribble Relay*

Select two classmates to participate with you in this exercise. You and one classmate stand on the goal line while the other player is positioned 30 yards away facing you. Begin the exercise with possession of the soccer ball. Start the relay by dribbling the 30-yard distance at maximum speed and exchanging possession of the ball with your classmate. Remain at that position and rest while your classmate immediately dribbles and exchanges the ball with the third player. The third player continues the circuit as he or she dribbles the ball back to you. Continue the exercise until all players have completed 20 repetitions of dribbling the ball the 30-yard distance. Award yourself 1 point for each time you dribble the 30-yard distance and exchange possession of the ball with a teammate without error. An error occurs if the ball bounces out of your range of control as you exchange possession with a classmate.

Success Goal = 18 of a possible 20 points

Your Score = (#) _____ points

7. *Dribble and Shield in the Grid*

The objective of this exercise is to shield the ball from an opponent within a 10-by-10-yard grid. The opponent marks or guards you tightly but applies only passive pressure; he or she plays as your ''shadow.'' The shadow does not try to win possession of the ball but merely applies pressure so you can practice readjusting your body to protect the ball. Remember to maintain sufficient space between the ball and your opponent at all times, and always control the ball with the foot farthest from the opponent. Play for 90 seconds. Penalize yourself 1 point each time the ball leaves the grid or each time it rolls outside your range of control. Repeat the exercise five times.

Success Goal = fewer than 15 penalty points in five 90-second drills

Your Score = (#) _____ penalty points

8. *Protect Your Ball*

Use the same basic setup as in the previous drill. In this exercise, however, your opponent applies maximum pressure in an attempt to win possession of the ball. You are penalized 1 point if the opponent gains possession of the ball or kicks it out of the grid. If the opponent gains possession of the ball he or she immediately returns it to you and the game continues. Play for 60 seconds and keep track of your penalty points. Take a 30-second rest, then reverse roles as you become the defender. Play for 60 seconds. The player with the lesser number of penalty points wins the competition.

Success Goal = fewer penalty points than opponent

Your Score =

    (#) _____ your penalty points

    (#) _____ opponent's penalty points

Individual Ball Possession Skills Keys to Success Checklists

Someone evaluating your dribbling ability must focus on the elements common to all dribbling techniques as well as the results of your efforts. If you can consistently take on and beat defenders even with a style that appears unorthodox, then your dribbling skills are fine. Remember that dribbling is an individual art that can vary from one player to the next. Ask your teacher, your coach, or a knowledgeable classmate to observe your dribbling ability in restricted space and open space. The observer can use the checklists in Figure 3.1 to evaluate your performance and provide corrective feedback.

Also ask your teacher, coach, or a classmate to observe your shielding technique. The observer should pay particular attention to your body positioning and your ability to unbalance the opponent through deceptive body movements. The checklist in Figure 3.2 can be used to evaluate your ability to shield the ball under pressure of an opponent.

Step 4   Gaining Possession of the Ball

To take the ball away from an opponent, you must develop your tackling skills. The term *tackle* has a different meaning in soccer than it does in American football. In soccer it means to use your feet to take the ball away from an opponent. Unlike the skills you've already learned, tackling is strictly a defensive skill used when you attempt to gain possession of the ball from an opponent.

Three types of tackles are commonly used depending on the game situation—the *block tackle*, *poke tackle*, and *slide tackle*. The block tackle is the preferred technique and is usually used when you are trying to tackle the ball from an opponent who is dribbling directly at you. The block tackle has several advantages over the poke and slide tackles. It provides a greater degree of body control and puts you in a position to quickly counterattack after winning possession of the ball. If you miss the tackle and fail to win possession of the ball, you are still in a position to quickly recover and chase the opponent.

WHY ARE TACKLING SKILLS IMPORTANT?

Tackling is essential in soccer. You must be able to gain possession of the ball to score goals and prevent the opponents from scoring. All field players regardless of position must be able to successfully execute tackling skills because each must assume defensive responsibilities when the opposing team has the ball.

HOW TO EXECUTE THE BLOCK TACKLE

Close the distance between you and the dribbler. Proper footwork is very important. As you prepare to tackle, position your feet in a staggered stance with one foot slightly ahead of the other. Assume a slightly crouched position with your knees flexed and your arms out to the sides for balance. This posture gives you a low center of gravity, which will enable you to react quickly to the dribbler's movements. At the opportune moment tackle the ball by blocking it with the inside surface of your foot. Keep your foot firmly positioned as you contact the ball. It is essential that you always attempt to play the ball when tackling an opponent. If in the judgment of the referee you are intentionally playing the person, then you will be signaled for a violation of the laws of play (see Figure 4.1a-b).

HOW TO EXECUTE THE POKE TACKLE

The poke tackle, also an effective means of dispossessing an opponent of the ball, is generally used to tackle the ball when you are approaching an opponent from his or her side. Reach in with your leg, extend your foot, and poke the ball away with your toes. Remember to play the ball, not the player. Kicking your opponent while trying to set the ball free is a foul (see Figure 4.1c-d).

HOW TO EXECUTE THE SLIDE TACKLE

The slide tackle is generally used as a last resort when the block and poke tackles are not possible. It is most appropriate when an opponent has beaten you on the dribble and there is no hope of catching him or her. Your only course of action is to kick the ball away in any direction possible.

In most instances you will use the slide tackle when chasing a dribbler from behind or the side. The technique looks quite similar to that of a baseball player sliding into a base. Leave your feet as you near the ball and slide on your side to a position slightly ahead of the ball. At the same time extend your lower leg and kick the ball away from the dribbler using the instep of your foot. Be sure that you do not make body contact with the opponent when you slide into the ball; you must contact the ball first. As a general rule, use the slide tackle sparingly. Because you must leave your feet in the attempt to kick the ball, you will be in a poor position to recover should you miss the tackle (see Figure 4.1e-g).

Figure 4.1   Keys to Success: Tackling

Preparation Phase

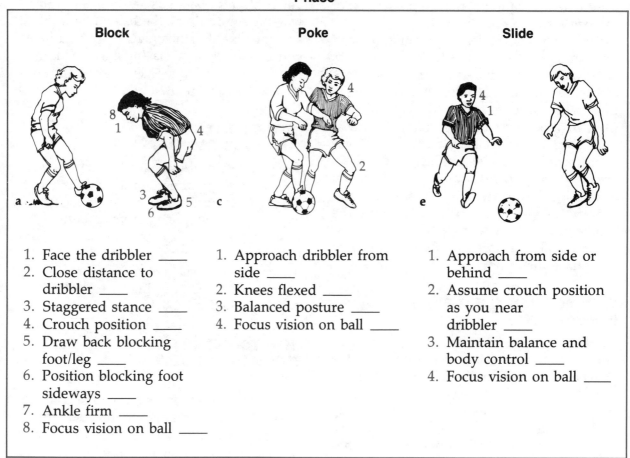

| Block | Poke | Slide |

1. Face the dribbler ____
2. Close distance to dribbler ____
3. Staggered stance ____
4. Crouch position ____
5. Draw back blocking foot/leg ____
6. Position blocking foot sideways ____
7. Ankle firm ____
8. Focus vision on ball ____

1. Approach dribbler from side ____
2. Knees flexed ____
3. Balanced posture ____
4. Focus vision on ball ____

1. Approach from side or behind ____
2. Assume crouch position as you near dribbler ____
3. Maintain balance and body control ____
4. Focus vision on ball ____

Execution
Phase

Block

Poke

Slide

1. Shoulders square ____
2. Momentum forward ____
3. Drive blocking foot into ball ____
4. Blocking foot firm ____
5. Contact center of ball ____
6. Maintain low center of gravity ____

1. Extend leg toward ball ____
2. Extend tackling foot ____
3. Poke ball with toes ____
4. Avoid contact with opponent ____

1. Leave feet ____
2. Slide on side ____
3. Place arms to side for balance ____
4. Extend sliding (lower) leg ahead of ball ____
5. Extend blocking foot ____
6. Other leg flexed at knee ____
7. Snap sliding leg/foot into ball ____
8. Contact ball on instep ____

**Follow-Through
Phase**

Block	Poke	Slide
1. Drive foot through point of contact ____	1. Withdraw leg ____	1. Avoid body contact with dribbler ____
2. Push ball forward past opponent ____	2. Chase the ball ____	2. Jump to feet ____
3. Gain possession ____	3. Collect ball if possible ____	3. Gain possession of ball if possible ____
4. Initiate counterattack ____		

Detecting Tackling Errors

Tackling skills are sometimes difficult to successfully execute. Most errors result from poor timing and improper technique. Remember to keep your body compact, get close to the dribbler, and then tackle the ball with power and determination. Common tackling errors are listed here along with suggested methods of correcting them.

ERROR

CORRECTION

Block Tackle

1. You lack sufficient strength and power when you block tackle the ball.

2. You block the ball with your foot but fail to push it past your opponent and gain possession.

1. Maintain good body control at all times. Keep your body compact and in a crouched position. Block the ball with a short, powerful snap of your leg. Do not extend your leg as you reach in to tackle. In that position you are susceptible to injury and, should you miss the tackle, will be unable to quickly recover to chase the dribbler.

2. Keep your foot and ankle firmly positioned as you block the ball. You cannot tackle the ball with authority and power if your foot shifts position.

ERROR 🚫

CORRECTION

Poke Tackle

1. You foul the opponent when you attempt to dispossess him or her of the ball.

1. Focus your vision on the ball so you do not get fooled by the opponent's body movements. Move to a position near your opponent, get a clear view of the ball, and then extend your leg and foot as you execute the tackle.

Slide Tackle

1. You foul the dribbler from behind when you attempt to slide into the ball.

1. Do not attempt to slide from directly behind the dribbler. Slide past him or her and try to hook your leg around to kick the ball. Remember, you have committed a foul if you initiate contact with the opponent without first touching the ball.

Tackling Drills

1. Block Tackle Stationary Ball

Have a classmate pin the ball to the ground with his or her foot while you practice the block tackle technique on a stationary ball. Assume the crouch position, firmly position your blocking foot sideways, and contact the center of the ball with the inside surface of your foot. Alternate using your right and left feet to block the ball. Execute 20 repetitions of the block tackle with each foot. Award yourself 1 point for each correct repetition of the block tackle technique.

Success Goals =

20 correct repetitions with right foot

20 correct repetitions with left foot

Your Score =

(#) ＿＿ points with right foot

(#) ＿＿ points with left foot

2. Block Tackle the Dribbler

Have a classmate dribble toward you at approximately half speed from a distance of 10 yards. Close the distance between you and the dribbler, assume the proper defensive posture, and block tackle the ball at the opportune moment. Concentrate on correct technique with good body control. Stay compact and low to the ground; do not extend your leg and do not lean backward as you block the ball. Block the ball with a short, powerful motion of your lower leg. Repeat for 10 repetitions with each foot, then switch roles with your classmate. Award yourself 1 point for each successful block tackle for a possible total of 10 points with each foot.

Success Goals =

   8 of 10 successful block tackles with right foot

   8 of 10 successful block tackles with left foot

Your Score =

   (#) ____ of 10 points with right foot

   (#) ____ of 10 points with left foot

3. Line-to-Line Game

Play against a classmate in a rectangular grid measuring 10 by 20 yards. Position yourself on one endline of the grid with your classmate standing on the opposite endline. Begin the drill by serving a ball to your opponent. His or her objective is to receive the ball, dribble it the length of the grid, and then stop the ball on your endline. Your objective is to prevent the opponent from dribbling to the endline by tackling the ball. Play at game speed. You are awarded 1 point each time you successfully tackle the ball away from your opponent. Use both the block tackle and poke tackle techniques. Repeat 10 times with each type of tackle, then switch roles so your opponent can practice his or her tackling skills.

Success Goal = 15 of 20 possible points

Your Score =

   (#) ____ points block tackle

   (#) ____ points poke tackle

4. All Against All

Select three classmates to participate with you in this exercise. Each of you has possession of a ball within the center circle of the soccer field or a similar-sized area. The objective is for each player to maintain possession of his or her ball while attempting to tackle and kick the other players' balls out of the playing area. Use dribbling and shielding skills to maintain possession of your ball; use block and poke tackles to dispossess opponents of their balls.

Slide tackles are not permitted due to the potential for injury in a crowded space. A player is awarded 1 point for each ball that he or she tackles and kicks out of the playing area. If your ball is kicked out of the playing area, quickly retrieve it and continue to play. Play the game for 5 minutes and keep track of your points.

Success Goal = score more points than your opponents

Your Score =

   (#) ＿＿ your points

   (#) ＿＿ opponent 1's points

   (#) ＿＿ opponent 2's points

   (#) ＿＿ opponent 3's points

5. Tackle All

All your classmates can participate with you in this exercise. Use cones or tape to mark off a grid area measuring approximately 20 by 20 yards. Select one classmate as your opponent and position yourself with him or her outside the grid area without soccer balls. All the other classmates, each with a ball, are positioned within the grid area. All players within the grid begin dribbling their balls. You and your opponent enter the area and individually attempt to tackle and win possession of a classmate's ball. If you do, that classmate is eliminated from the exercise. Then attempt to tackle and win another classmate's ball. Continue until all the dribblers have been eliminated from the game. You and your opponent are awarded 1 point for each ball successfully tackled.

Success Goal = score more points than your opponent

Your Score =

   (#) ＿＿ your points

   (#) ＿＿ opponent's points

Tackling Skills
Keys to Success Checklist

Ask your teacher, your coach, or a classmate to observe your tackling skills. Begin with the block tackle, then progress to the poke and slide tackles as you become more confident.

The observer can use the checklist in Figure 4.1 to evaluate your performance and provide corrective feedback.

Step 5 Individual Attack and Defense Tactics

Whereas soccer skills require precise execution of various movements, soccer tactics encompass the strategies and decision-making processes used when attacking and defending on an individual, small group, and team basis. You will be confronted with many options during a game, such as whether to dribble or pass the ball, the type of pass to use, whether to tackle or contain, and where to position yourself when not in possession of the ball. The ability to make correct decisions is just as important to your success as proper execution of soccer skills. To improve your decision-making ability you must develop knowledge and understanding of soccer tactics. It is best if you start with the most basic tactical unit—one player versus one player.

WHY ARE INDIVIDUAL ATTACKING AND DEFENDING TACTICS IMPORTANT?

The foundation of soccer tactics is the one-versus-one situation that occurs so often during a typical match. Soccer, much like basketball, requires that all field players be able to defend as well as attack. When you have possession of the ball you are the attacker; when the opponent you are marking has possession of the ball you are the defender. Whichever team's players win the majority of these one-versus-one confrontations usually wins the game. To enjoy personal success as well as contribute to your team as a whole, you must understand the basic principles associated with individual attack and defense.

Your ability to choose the correct course of action from a multitude of options is critical when you are confronted by a defending opponent. Even if you are physically superior to the opponent, if you consistently make the wrong decisions you will probably not enjoy success, and your team will suffer the consequences.

HOW TO EXECUTE INDIVIDUAL ATTACK TACTICS

When you have possession of the ball use the following general guidelines for making your decisions.

Maintain Ball Possession

First and foremost you must not lose possession of the ball to the opponent (Figure 5.1a). Obviously your team cannot score without the ball, and each loss of possession presents the opposing team with a potential scoring opportunity.

Create Space for Yourself

In soccer an important equation always holds true: Space equals time. The more space you create between you and the opponent marking you, the more time you will have to make decisions and play the ball. By creating space for yourself you become a better player.

You can create space between you and an opponent in two ways—using deceptive body feints and using checking runs. Body feints are movements that unbalance the opponent. A slight dip of your shoulder or a quick step over the ball may be all that is needed (Figure 5.1b). A checking run is a short, quick burst of speed designed to fool the defender into thinking that you are planning to dribble past him or her. Take a step toward the defender as if to go by him or her, then quickly push the ball in the opposite direction.

Turn On the Defender

Mere possession of the ball does not guarantee successful attacking soccer. Your ultimate objective is to score goals. Toward that aim you must position yourself to attack the opponent's goal whenever possible. For example, you may receive and control a ball while you are positioned with your back to the opponent's goal. Even though you have possession of the ball, the advantage still lies with the defending player because you are facing your own goal and are not in a dangerous scoring position. In that situation you should try to turn with the ball and face the opponent's goal. Before attempting to turn, however, first create space between you and the opponent marking you (Figure 5.1c).

Take On the Defender

Immediately dribble at the defender once you have turned with the ball. This is commonly referred to as *taking on* the defender. By doing this you have shifted the burden of responsibility. The defender must now decide whether to tackle the ball or retreat. If the defending player makes the wrong decision you may have an opportunity to score or set up a score for a teammate.

Take on an opponent only in certain situations and areas of the field. Do not attempt to take on and dribble past an opponent in the defending third of the field nearest your own goal. Loss of possession in that area can result in a goal against your team. Always think ''safety first'' in your own end of the field. For the most part you should use your dribbling skills to take on opponents in the attacking third of the field nearest the opponent's goal. You can risk losing possession in that area in an attempt to create a scoring opportunity for your team.

Take the Shortest Route to the Goal

When taking on an opponent follow the shortest, most direct route to the goal. If you have the option, try to beat the defender to his or her inside rather than dribbling wide around him or her. Goals are usually scored from central areas that provide a wide shooting angle to the goal. The shooting angle narrows as you move toward the flank areas.

Figure 5.1 *Keys to Success: Individual Attack Tactics*

Maintain Ball Possession

1. Position body between opponent and ball ____
2. Control with foot farthest from opponent ____
3. React to pressure of defender ____

a

Create Space
for Yourself

1. Use body feints to un-
   balance opponent ____
2. Use checking runs ____
3. Use quick changes of
   direction ____

b

Turn On
Defender

1. Protect the ball ____
2. Create space in which to
   turn ____
3. Turn on defender ____

c

Take On
Defender

1. Face defender ____
2. Dribble at defender ____
3. Commit defender to
   you ____

4. React to defender's
   actions ____

Shortest Route
to Goal

1. Beat defender to his or
   her inside if
   possible ____

2. Penetrate defense ____
3. Create a wide shooting
   angle to goal ____

HOW TO EXECUTE INDIVIDUAL DEFENSE TACTICS

Defensive soccer is based on the philosophy of little or no risk. You cannot afford to take chances on defense because even a small miscalculation can result in an opponent's score. Aim to avoid giving up goals as a result of defensive mistakes. If an opposing player scores a goal, let it be due to his or her good play rather than your poor play. As with individual attacking tactics, your decision-making abilities play a critical role in your overall performance. Use the following principles as a basis for your decisions when defending in a one-versus-one situation.

Control/Balance

Remember that an opponent with the ball will use deceptive feints and body movements to unbalance you, to get you leaning one way or another. Always strive to maintain good balance and body control so you can quickly react to the dribbler's every movement.

Approach to the Ball

Quickly close the distance between you and the player you are marking when you see that he or she is about to receive a pass from a teammate. Slow your approach as you near the opponent so you maintain balance and body control. Ideally you should arrive at about the same moment as the ball. Remember that space equals time: The less space you allow your opponent, the less time he or she has to make decisions and play the ball.

Defensive Stance

Assume a slightly crouched posture with a low center of gravity. Use a staggered stance with your feet approximately shoulder-width apart and one foot slightly forward of the other (Figure 5.2a). A staggered stance enables you to quickly change direction in response to the opponent's movements.

Marking Distance

How close to an opponent you should position yourself when defending in a one-versus-one situation depends on several factors. Base your decision on the following:

- *Ability of the opponent.* Give the opponent a bit more space if he or she has great speed and quickness. This will prevent the opponent from merely pushing the ball past you and outracing you to it. If the opponent is not exceptionally fast but instead relies on a high degree of skill, you should mark the player very tightly so as to limit the space and time he or she has available (Figure 5.2b).
- *Area of the field.* As a general rule of thumb, the closer an opponent is to your goal, the tighter he or she should be marked. An opponent within scoring range of your goal must be denied the opportunity to shoot or pass the ball forward.
- *Position of the ball with relation to the player you are marking.* Give your opponent more space as he or she moves farther away from the position of the ball. Your marking distance should be such that if the ball is passed to the opponent you are marking, you can close the distance between you and the opponent while the ball is in flight. Always position yourself to keep the ball and your opponent within your range of vision.

Goalside Position

Your defensive position in relation to the opponent, the ball, and your goal is very important. Always position yourself goalside, between the opponent and the goal you are defending. It is also to your advantage to position yourself slightly to the inside of the player you are marking, shading him or her toward the center of the field. From the inside position you can shut off the dribbler's most direct route to the goal.

Prevent the Turn

Once your opponent has received and controlled the ball with his or her back to you, try to prevent him or her from turning to face you. If the opponent turns with the ball and faces you, he or she will be able to serve penetrating passes into the space behind you or attempt to beat you on the dribble. You will maintain the advantage as long as you keep the opponent facing his or her own goal.

Containment

Occasionally an opponent will successfully turn on you with the ball. If so, you should position yourself to delay his or her forward movement. Try to channel the opponent into areas where space is limited (i.e., toward the sideline or into a nearby teammate).

Tackle the Ball

If you have followed the basic principles of individual defense to this point, you should be in an excellent position to challenge for possession of the ball. At the opportune moment tackle and gain possession of the ball.

Figure 5.2 Keys to Success:
Individual Defense Tactics

Control/Balance

1. Weight centered over balls of feet ____

2. Knees slightly flexed ____
3. Arms out to sides ____

Approach to the Ball

1. Anticipate pass to player you are marking ____
2. Move toward your opponent ____
3. Close distance while ball is in flight ____

4. Slow your run as you near opponent ____
5. Maintain body control and balance ____

Defensive Stance

1. Crouched posture ____
2. Weight centered ____
3. Arms to sides ____
4. Feet approximately shoulder-width apart ____
5. Staggered stance ____
6. Vision focused on ball ____

a

Marking Distance

1. Make judgment of opponent's ability ____
2. Consider area of field ____
3. Consider position of ball in relation to opponent ____
4. Tighter marking of opponent nearer your goal area ____
5. Looser marking in opponent's half of field ____
6. Tighter marking if ball is near opponent ____
7. Looser marking if opponent is far from ball ____

b

Goalside Position

1. Position goalside of opponent ____
2. Position inside of opponent ____
3. Keep ball in view at all times ____

Prevent the Turn

1. Tight marking ____
2. Vision on ball ____
3. Maintain balance and body control ____

Containment

1. Delay forward movement of dribbler ____
2. Do not become reckless and overcommit ____
3. Force dribbler toward sideline ____
4. Force dribbler into covering teammate ____

Tackle the Ball

1. Maintain balance and body control ____
2. Close marking distance ____
3. Vision focused on ball ____
4. Crouched position ____
5. Tackle the ball ____

Detecting Errors in Individual Attack and Defense Tactics

Because tactics deal with decision making as well as skill execution, the errors listed here are conceptual rather than biomechanical. Common errors that occur with individual attacking and defending tactics are listed along with suggestions for avoiding or correcting them.

ERROR

CORRECTION

Individual Attack Tactics

1. The defender challenges for possession and tackles the ball away from you.

2. You fail to successfully turn with the ball and face the defender.

3. You turn on the opponent but delay in taking him or her on. Your hesitation gives other defenders time to recover and position themselves between you and the goal.

1. Use your body to shield and protect the ball at all times.

2. Use body feints, checking runs, or both to create space between you and the opponent before turning with the ball.

3. Be decisive. Take on the defending player immediately after turning with the ball.

Individual Defense Tactics

1. You permit the attacking player to turn with the ball and face you.

2. You overcommit in an effort to win the ball and are beaten on the dribble.

3. The attacking player passes the ball past you into the open space behind you.

1. Deny your opponent the space necessary to turn with the ball. Tight marking is essential.

2. Maintain good balance at all times. Position your feet in a staggered stance with your weight evenly distributed. Do not attempt to tackle the ball until you are fairly sure you can successfully win possession.

3. This occurs because your marking distance is too great. Step up and reduce the distance between you and the opponent with the ball. As you move forward the opponent will not be able to pass the ball directly forward, but rather will have to pass it square or back to a supporting teammate.

Individual Attack and Defense Drills

1. Keep Away

Play with a classmate within a 10-by-10-yard grid area. Begin with possession of the ball while your classmate plays as the defender. Use body feints coupled with dribbling and shielding skills to maintain possession of the ball from the defender within the grid area. Try to maintain ball possession for 10 seconds, then rest. Award yourself 1 point each time you can maintain possession of the ball for 10 seconds. Award the defender 1 point each time he or she tackles the ball away from you. Repeat the exercise 10 times, then switch roles with the defender and repeat 10 more times.

Success Goals =

6 or more of 10 possible points as attacker

6 or more of 10 possible points as defender

Your Score =

(#) _____ attacking points

(#) _____ defending points

2. Receive Under Pressure

Play within a 10-by-10-yard grid area. Position a classmate directly behind you as a defender. A server with a supply of soccer balls faces you at a distance of 15 yards from the grid. Receive passes from the server while being challenged from behind by the defender. Shield and protect the ball as you receive it. Try to maintain possession of the ball for 10 seconds, then return it to the server. Repeat 10 times. Award yourself 1 point each time you receive, control, and maintain possession of the ball within the grid for 10 seconds. Award the defender 1 point each time he or she wins possession of the ball. After 10 repetitions of the exercise, switch roles with the defender.

Success Goals =

7 of 10 possible points as attacker

7 of 10 possible points as defender

Your Score =

(#) _____ attacking points

(#) _____ defending points

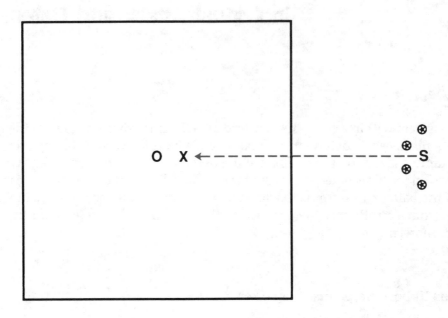

3. Receive and Turn

The drill proceeds in the same manner as the previous one except that you are awarded 1 point each time you receive, control, and turn with the ball to face the defender within the 10-by-10-yard grid. You have 10 seconds in which to receive the ball and turn. The defender is awarded 1 point each time he or she prevents you from turning with the ball within 10 seconds. Repeat 10 times, then switch roles with the defender and repeat.

Success Goals =

6 of 10 possible points as attacker

8 of 10 possible points as defender

Your Score =

(#) _____ attacking points

(#) _____ defending points

4. Receive, Turn, and Dribble

The drill proceeds in the same manner as the previous two. You are awarded 1 point each time you successfully turn with the ball and face the defender. You are awarded 1 additional point if you beat the defender by dribbling past him or her within the confines of the 10-by-10-yard grid. You have 10 seconds to receive the ball, turn, and take on the defender. The defender is awarded 2 points if he or she prevents you from turning with the ball. Repeat 10 times for a maximum possible total of 20 points each, then switch roles and repeat.

Success Goals =

  12 of 20 possible points as attacker

  14 of 20 possible points as defender

Your Score =

  (#) ____ attacking points

  (#) ____ defending points

5. *One Versus One to a Central Goal*

Play one versus one with a classmate within a 15-by-15-yard grid area. Your classmate has possession of the ball, and you play as the defender. Place a cone in the center of the grid to represent a common goal. Your objective is to prevent your classmate from beating you on the dribble and passing his or her ball to hit the cone. Your classmate is awarded 1 point if he or she beats you on the dribble, and 1 additional point if he or she hits the cone with the ball. You are awarded 1 point if you successfully tackle and win possession of the ball. If you win possession of the ball, immediately return it to your opponent and continue the exercise. Play continuously for 5 minutes, keeping track of points scored. Switch roles and repeat the exercise after a short rest.

Success Goals =

  as attacker score more points than defender

  as defender score more points than attacker

Your Score =

  (#) ____ your attacking points   (#) ____ opponent's defending points

  (#) ____ your defending points   (#) ____ opponent's attacking points

6. *Defend the Line*

Stand on the goal line with a ball midway between the goalposts. Pass the ball to a classmate standing 25 yards from the goal. Immediately move forward from the goal line after passing the ball and play as a defender; your classmate attempts to dribble the ball past you. You are awarded 1 point if you successfully tackle and gain possession of the ball; your classmate is awarded 1 point if he or she dribbles past you to the goal line. Repeat 20 times, then switch roles with your classmate.

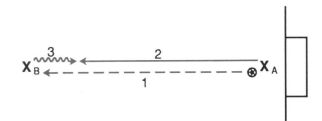

Success Goals =

as attacker score more points than defender

as defender score more points than attacker

Your Score =

(#) _____ your attacking points   (#) _____ opponent's defending points

(#) _____ your defending points   (#) _____ opponent's attacking points

7. One Versus One With Goals

Select a classmate to participate with you in this exercise. Play one versus one in a 10-by-20-yard grid area. Use cones or flags to designate a small goal (2 yards wide) at each end of the grid. Flip a coin to decide who has possession of the ball to begin the game. You score 1 point each time you beat your opponent and pass the ball through his or her goal. The opponent scores in the same manner by passing the ball through your goal. Do not use goalkeepers. Play continuously, changing possession of the ball after each point scored. Continue the game until one player scores 10 points.

Success Goal = score 10 points before your opponent does

Your Score =

(#) _____ your points

(#) _____ opponent's points

Individual Attack Tactics
Keys to Success Checklists

Ask your teacher, your coach, or a classmate to observe you in one-versus-one practice situations. The observer should focus his or her attention on your decision-making abilities and determine whether you are executing the appropriate behavior(s) for each given situation. The observer should use the checklists in Figures 5.1 and 5.2 to evaluate your performance.

Step 6 Heading Skills

Heading skills are unique to the sport of soccer. Soccer is the only game in which players literally "use their heads" to propel the ball. Heading skills can be used to pass the ball to teammates, to score goals, and for defensive clearances around the goal area.

Two types of heading skills are used in game competition. The *jump header* is generally used to pass or shoot the ball in the offensive end of the field, or it can be used to clear the ball out of your goal area in the defensive end of the field. The *dive header* is an exciting and acrobatic skill used only on special occasions; for instance, to score spectacular goals off low crosses. Do not use the dive header when in a crowd of players, however. Someone may accidentally kick you in the face or head when trying to play the ball. Use good judgment!

WHY ARE HEADING SKILLS IMPORTANT?

To become a complete soccer player, one who can play the ball on the ground as well as in the air, you must develop good heading skills. Goal kicks, corner kicks, lofted passes, and defensive clearances must often be played directly out of the air with your head.

HOW TO EXECUTE THE JUMP HEADER

Prepare to execute the jump header in much the same manner as when you receive a ball with your head. Face the ball as it descends. Use a two-footed takeoff to jump up. While in the air arch your upper body back and tuck your chin toward your chest. Keep your neck firm and your vision focused on the ball. Snap your upper body forward and contact the ball on your forehead at the highest point of your jump. Keep your eyes open and mouth closed as you head the ball. Heading the ball with your mouth open invites injury because you may bite your tongue if you get bumped by an opponent who is also jumping for the ball (see Figure 6.1a-c).

HOW TO EXECUTE THE DIVE HEADER

The dive header is used to head a ball that is traveling parallel to the ground at waist level or lower. Face the ball and assume a slightly crouched position. Judge the velocity of the ball, anticipate its arrival, and then dive parallel to the ground to meet it. Tilt your head back and keep your eyes open, mouth closed, and neck firm as you contact the ball on your forehead. Extend your arms downward to break your fall to the ground (see Figure 6.1d-e).

Figure 6.1 Keys to Success: Heading

Preparation Phase

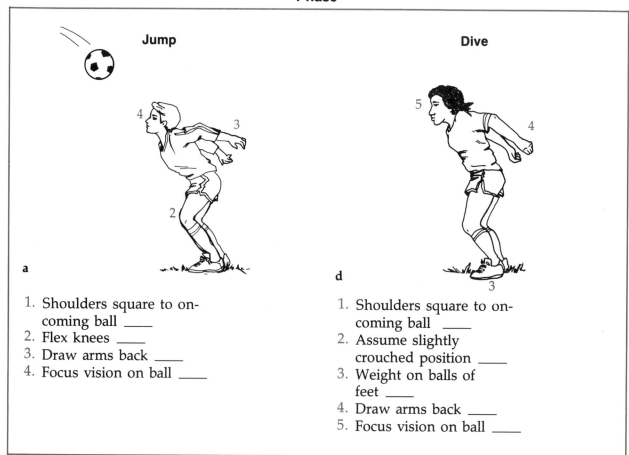

Jump

a

1. Shoulders square to on-coming ball ____
2. Flex knees ____
3. Draw arms back ____
4. Focus vision on ball ____

Dive

d

1. Shoulders square to on-coming ball ____
2. Assume slightly crouched position ____
3. Weight on balls of feet ____
4. Draw arms back ____
5. Focus vision on ball ____

Execution Phase

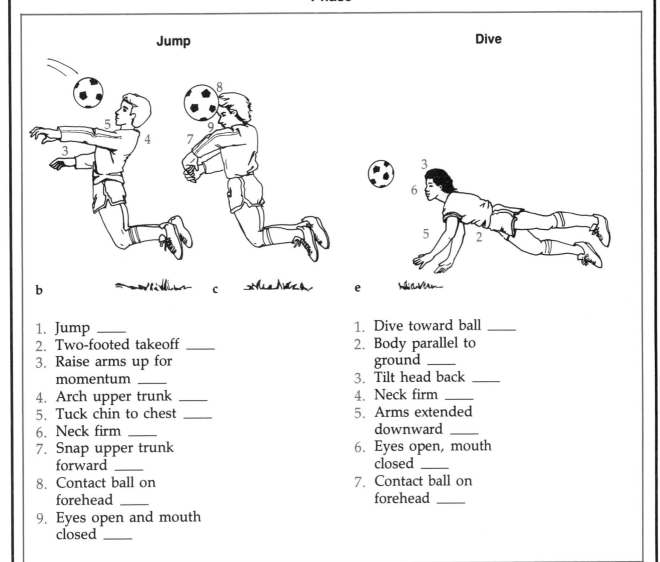

Jump

Dive

b   c   e

1. Jump ____
2. Two-footed takeoff ____
3. Raise arms up for momentum ____
4. Arch upper trunk ____
5. Tuck chin to chest ____
6. Neck firm ____
7. Snap upper trunk forward ____
8. Contact ball on forehead ____
9. Eyes open and mouth closed ____

1. Dive toward ball ____
2. Body parallel to ground ____
3. Tilt head back ____
4. Neck firm ____
5. Arms extended downward ____
6. Eyes open, mouth closed ____
7. Contact ball on forehead ____

Follow-Through Phase

Jump

Dive

1. Drive forehead through point of contact ____
2. Follow through motion with upper trunk ____
3. Arms out to sides for balance ____
4. Land softly on ground with both feet ____

1. Momentum forward through point of contact ____
2. Watch flight of ball ____
3. Break fall with arms ____
4. Jump to feet ____

Detecting Heading Errors

Correct execution of heading skills requires coordination of movement as well as precise timing. Beginners often have difficulty combining all elements of the techniques simultaneously. Don't get discouraged; remember that practice makes perfect. Common heading errors are listed here along with suggestions for correcting them.

ERROR

CORRECTION

Jump Header

1. The ball does not travel in the direction that you wanted it to.

2. You fail to meet the ball at the highest point of your jump.

3. You do not transfer sufficient power to the headed ball.

Dive Header

1. Your header lacks power and accuracy.

2. The ball pops up off your head.

1. You are probably failing to contact the ball on your forehead. The large, flat surface of your forehead provides the best surface with which to head the ball. Remember to square your shoulders with the oncoming ball. Keep your neck and head firmly positioned as you contact the ball.

2. Timing your jump may be the most critical element of successful heading skills. Most beginners tend to jump too late. As a result, they are still moving upward as the ball arrives. Try to jump early, hang in the air for an instant, and then snap forward to meet the oncoming ball.

3. You are probably failing to snap your upper body and head forward as you impact the ball. You must attack the ball, not let it attack you. Try to maintain the arched position until the last instant, then powerfully drive your upper body and head forward to contact the ball.

1. Keep your neck firm and head steady as you dive toward the ball. Contact the ball on the flat surface of your forehead.

2. This occurs because you contact the ball too high on your forehead. Do not dip your head as the ball arrives; keep it firmly positioned and contact the ball on the center of your forehead.

Heading Drills

1. Head Ball to Hands

Hold a ball at approximately head height with both hands. Softly toss the ball off your forehead and nod it back into your hands. Keep your eyes open, mouth closed, neck firm, and chin tucked to chest. Repeat 30 times.

Success Goal = 30 of 30 balls headed directly back into your hands

Your Score = (#) _____ of 30 balls

2. Heading From Knees

Kneel facing a classmate standing 2 yards away. Have your classmate toss a ball toward your head. Arch your upper body backward and head the ball to the classmate, who catches the ball and repeats the drill. Keep your eyes open, mouth closed, and neck rigid, and snap your upper body forward as you head the ball. Repeat 30 times, then change roles with your classmate.

Success Goal = 27 of 30 tosses headed directly to classmate

Your Score = (#) _____ of 30 tosses headed directly to classmate

3. Jump and Head Stationary Ball

Stand facing a classmate approximately 12 to 18 inches away. The classmate holds a ball above and to the front of his or her head. Jump straight up, arch your upper body, and snap forward to contact the ball on your forehead. Combine all elements of the jump header technique. Repeat 30 times, then switch roles with your partner.

Success Goal = 25 of 30 balls contacted on your forehead

Your Score = (#) _____ of 30 balls contacted

4. Jump Header to Partner

Face a classmate 5 yards away. The classmate tosses a ball to a point approximately 1 foot above your head. Jump and head the ball back to the classmate. Attempt to contact the ball on the center of your forehead at the highest point of your jump. Repeat 20 times, then switch roles.

Success Goal = 17 of 20 tosses headed directly to classmate's chest

Your Score = (#) _____ of 20 tosses headed to classmate's chest

5. Moving Headers

Use the same setup as in the previous drill except that you and the classmate are slowly jogging. The classmate jogs slowly backward while you move toward the ball as you head it. Remember to jump, arch your upper body back, and snap forward as you contact the ball on your forehead. The added pressure of movement makes it more difficult to successfully execute the skill. Head 20 tosses, then switch roles.

Success Goal = 15 of 20 tosses headed to classmate's chest

Your Score = (#) _____ of 20 tosses headed to classmate's chest

6. Head, Catch, and Throw

Form a triangle with two classmates, with about 10 yards between players. Designate yourself as number 1 and your classmates numbers 2 and 3. Begin the exercise by tossing the ball to player 2 who jumps and heads the ball to player 3. Player 3 catches the ball in his or her hands and tosses it to you. You jump and head the ball to player 2 who catches it and tosses to player 3. Continue the head-catch-throw circuit until each player has headed the ball 20 times. Try to head each toss directly to the appropriate player so that the ball does not fall to the ground.

Success Goal = 16 of 20 tosses headed to classmate

Your Score = (#) _____ of 20 tosses headed to classmate

7. Diving Headers

Practice this drill on a landing pit used in track, a gymnastics mat, or any type of soft ground. Face a server approximately 10 yards away. The server tosses a ball toward you parallel to the ground at approximately waist height. Dive forward and head the ball back to the server using the dive header technique. Remember to extend your arms downward to cushion your fall. Repeat 10 times. Try to head each toss directly back to the server so he or she does not have to move more than one step in any direction to catch the ball.

Success Goal = 7 of 10 tosses headed directly to the server

Your Score = (#) _____ of 10 tosses headed directly to the server

Heading Skills
Keys to Success Checklist

Have your teacher, your coach, or a skilled classmate observe your jump heading and dive heading techniques. The observer should focus on several key aspects of performance for each skill. When executing the jump header, always try to contact the ball at the highest point of your jump. It is important that you hold your arched position until the last possible instant, then snap forward into the ball.

Your head and neck should be firmly positioned. When executing the dive header be sure to extend your body parallel to the ground as you dive forward. Tilt your head back, keep your neck firm, and contact the ball on your forehead. Use the checklist in Figure 6.1 to evaluate your performance and provide corrective feedback.

Step 7 Shooting Skills

Scoring goals is the single most difficult task in soccer as evidenced by the relatively few goals scored in a typical match. Players use a variety of shooting skills depending on whether the ball is rolling, bouncing, or dropping from the air. Basic shooting techniques include the *instep drive, full volley, half volley, side volley,* and *swerving* or *bending shots.* Your success in shooting depends on several factors. Obviously the ability to shoot with either foot under pressure from defending opponents is essential. You must also factor in qualities such as anticipation, determination, confidence, composure, and sometimes even a bit of luck. It is important that you practice shooting skills in situations that simulate actual game conditions.

WHY IS SHOOTING IMPORTANT?

The final objective of every attack is a goal scored. Scoring goals in actual game competition is not easy, however. To score goals on a regular basis you must be able to execute the various shooting skills under the game-related pressures of limited time, restricted space, physical fatigue, and opponents trying to deny you the shot.

HOW TO EXECUTE
THE INSTEP DRIVE SHOT

Use the instep drive to shoot a rolling or stationary ball. The technique is very similar to that used for the instep pass. Approach the ball from a slight angle. Plant your balance foot beside the ball with the knee of your balance leg slightly flexed. From this position your body will be over the ball as you kick it. Focus your vision on the ball. Draw your kicking leg back and extend your foot. Strike the center of the ball with the full instep of your kicking foot. Keep your kicking foot firmly positioned. Use a complete follow-through motion to generate maximum power on the shot (see Figure 7.1).

HOW TO EXECUTE
THE FULL VOLLEY SHOT

Use the full volley technique to shoot a ball directly out of the air. Face the ball with shoulders square. Draw your kicking leg back and extend the kicking foot. Keep your head steady and your vision on the ball. Snap your kicking leg forward from the knee and contact the ball with the full instep. Your kicking foot should be pointed down at the moment of contact, ensuring that your knee is positioned above the ball. Correct position of the foot and knee is required to keep the shot low. Use a powerful follow-through of the kicking motion to generate power on the shot (see Figure 7.2a-d).

HOW TO EXECUTE
THE HALF VOLLEY SHOT

The kicking technique for the half volley shot is quite similar to that used for the full volley. The primary difference is that the ball is volleyed not directly out of the air but rather at the instant it contacts the ground. To execute the half volley you must anticipate where the ball will drop to the ground and move to that spot. Face the ball with shoulders square. Draw your kicking leg back and fully extend the kicking foot. Snap your kicking leg forward and contact the ball with your instep at the moment the ball hits the ground. Use a short, powerful kicking motion, not a complete follow-through (see Figure 7.2e-g).

HOW TO EXECUTE
THE SIDE VOLLEY SHOT

Use the side volley to shoot a ball that is bouncing or dropping to the side of you. In preparing to shoot, turn your body sideways to the oncoming ball. Raise your kicking leg to the side so it is almost parallel to the ground. Draw back your kicking leg by flexing the knee. Extend your kicking foot. Keep your head steady and your vision focused on the ball. Snap your lower leg toward the ball and contact the top half of the ball with your instep. Keep your kicking foot firmly positioned throughout the entire motion (see Figure 7.2h-l).

HOW TO EXECUTE A SWERVING SHOT

Sometimes the straight path to the goal may not be the best route. Shots that curve in flight are often difficult to catch and may fool opposing goalkeepers. You can make your shot swerve in flight by imparting spin to the ball. Begin your approach from a position almost directly behind the ball. Plant your balance foot beside the ball, keeping your head steady and your vision on the ball. Draw back your kicking leg and extend the kicking foot. Use the inside or outside portion of your instep to contact the ball. Using your right foot, if you contact the outer half of the ball with the inside of your instep, the shot will curve inward. If you contact the inside half of the ball with the outside of your instep, then the shot will curve outward. Keep your kicking foot firmly positioned. A complete follow-through motion will give your shot greater power and swerve (see Figure 7.3).

Figure 7.1   Keys to Success: Instep Drive Shot

Preparation Phase

1. Approach ball from slight angle ____
2. Plant balance foot beside ball ____
3. Flex balance leg at knee ____
4. Arms out to sides for balance ____
5. Draw back kicking leg ____
6. Extend kicking foot ____
7. Head down and steady ____
8. Vision focused on ball ____

Execution
Phase

1. Square shoulders with target ____
2. Body over ball ____
3. Snap kicking leg forward ____
4. Kicking foot firm ____
5. Contact center of ball with instep ____

b

Follow-Through
Phase

1. Momentum forward ____
2. Rise up on ball of balance foot ____
3. Complete follow-through motion ____
4. Eyes follow flight of ball ____

c

Figure 7.2 Keys to Success:
Volley Shots

**Preparation
Phase**

Full Volley   **Half Volley**   **Side Volley**

a

e

h

i

1. Face ball with shoulders square ___
2. Flex balance leg ___
3. Draw back kicking leg ___
4. Extend kicking foot ___
5. Arms to sides for balance ___
6. Vision focused on ball ___

1. Face ball with shoulders square ___
2. Move to spot where ball will drop to ground ___
3. Flex balance leg ___
4. Draw back kicking leg ___
5. Extend kicking foot and keep firm ___
6. Arms to sides for balance ___
7. Head steady with vision on ball ___

1. Position body sideways to flight of ball ___
2. Weight on balance leg ___
3. Flex balance leg ___
4. Arms out to sides for balance ___
5. Raise kicking leg to side parallel to ground ___
6. Kicking leg drawn back, flexed at knee ___
7. Kicking foot extended ___
8. Vision focused on ball ___

Execution
Phase

Full Volley

b

c

Half Volley

f

Side Volley

j

1. Knee of kicking leg over ball ____
2. Snap kicking leg forward from knee ____
3. Kicking foot firm ____
4. Contact center of ball with instep ____

1. Knee of kicking leg over ball ____
2. Snap lower leg forward ____
3. Keep kicking foot firm ____
4. Kicking foot pointed down ____
5. Contact ball as it hits ground ____

1. Rotate half turn toward ball on balance foot ____
2. Snap kicking leg toward ball ____
3. Contact top half of ball with instep ____

Follow-Through
Phase

Full Volley	**Half Volley**	**Side Volley**

d

g

k

l

1. Kicking leg snaps straight ____
2. Momentum forward ____
3. Watch flight of ball ____

1. Kicking leg snaps straight ____
2. Momentum forward ____
3. Watch flight of ball ____

1. Kicking leg snaps straight ____
2. Angle kicking motion slightly downward ____
3. Drop kicking foot to ground ____
4. Watch flight of ball ____

Figure 7.3   Keys to Success:
Swerving Shots

**Preparation
Phase**

1. Approach from behind ball ____
2. Place balance foot beside ball ____
3. Flex balance leg ____
4. Draw back kicking leg ____
5. Extend kicking foot ____
6. Arms out to sides for balance ____
7. Vision focused on ball ____

a

**Execution
Phase**

1. Momentum forward ____
2. Contact ball left or right of its vertical midline ____
3. Use inside or outside of instep as kicking surface ____
4. Keep kicking foot firm ____

b

Follow-Through Phase

1. Drive foot through point of contact with ball ____
2. Use inside-out follow-through motion for outside of instep shot and outside-in follow-through motion for inside of instep shot ____
3. Follow-through motion to waist level or higher ____
4. Watch flight of ball ____

c

Detecting Shooting Errors

Common objectives of all shooting skills are accuracy, power, and a low trajectory. You are most likely to score off a low shot because it is most difficult for goalkeepers to dive and save low shots. Common shooting errors are listed here along with suggestions for correcting them.

ERROR    **CORRECTION**

Instep Drive, Full Volley, and Half Volley Shots

1. Your shot travels up over the goal.

1. Improper position of the balance foot is the most likely cause of this error. Plant your balance foot beside the ball, not behind it. Your kicking foot must be completely extended and your body must be over the ball at the moment of contact. Do not lean backward as you contact the ball.

2. Your shot lacks power.

2. Lack of power is usually due to insufficient follow-through motion of the kicking leg. Continue the follow-through motion until your kicking foot rises to approximately chest height.

ERROR	CORRECTION
3. You consistently pull your shot to either the right or the left of the goal.	3. Square your shoulders with the intended target as you kick the ball. Strike the ball with the full surface of your instep. Use a complete follow-through motion and watch the flight of the ball as it leaves your foot.
4. You fail to contact the ball on your instep.	4. This error results from taking your eye off the ball or, with the half volley, from kicking the ball after it has started to bounce up from the ground.

Side Volley Shot

1. Your shot lacks power and accuracy.	1. This error is usually due to an incorrect kicking motion. When possible, the knee of your kicking leg should be higher than the ball at the moment you kick it. From that position you can kick down through the top half of the ball, which will keep the shot low. Don't extend your kicking leg too soon; keep it in a cocked position until the last possible moment and then drive your foot into the ball with a short, powerful motion.

Swerving Shot

1. Your shot fails to curve in flight.	1. This occurs because you do not impart sufficient spin on the ball. Contact the ball to the left or the right of its vertical midline, not directly through its center. Use a complete follow-through motion.
2. Your shot lacks power.	2. Lack of power may be due to one of three reasons. Either you contact the ball too close to its outer edge, your foot is not firmly positioned as you kick the ball, or you do not follow through properly. You must keep your kicking foot firm and contact the ball just right or left of its center. Try to get as much of your instep on the ball as possible. A complete follow-through is required to generate power on the shot.

Shooting Drills

1. *Shoot the Wall*

Use masking tape to outline a regulation-size goal on a wall or kickboard. Attempt to shoot a stationary ball into the goal from a distance of 20 yards. Stop the ball each time it rebounds to you and then shoot again from that spot. Alternate shooting with left and right feet. Take 20 instep drive shots and 20 swerving shots. Award yourself 1 point for each shot on goal.

Success Goals =

16 of 20 points with instep drive shot

14 of 20 points with swerving shot

Your Score =

(#) ____ instep drive shot points

(#) ____ swerving shot points

2. *Shoot to a Partner*

Stand facing a classmate 10 yards away. Have the classmate roll a ball to you. Shoot the rolling ball back to your classmate using the instep drive and swerving shot techniques. Alternate shooting with left and right feet. Execute 20 repetitions with each type of shot, then switch roles with your classmate. Award yourself 1 point for each shot directly to your classmate.

Success Goals =

16 of 20 points with instep drive shot

14 of 20 points with swerving shot

Your Score =

(#) ____ instep drive shot points

(#) ____ swerving shot points

3. Shoot Through the Cones

Place two cones 8 yards apart, the width of a regulation goal. Position yourself with a ball 25 yards from the cones while a classmate is positioned 50 yards away from you on the opposite side of the cones. You have possession of the ball to begin the drill. Dribble forward 2 to 3 yards and then attempt to shoot the ball through the cones. Your classmate collects the ball and tries to score in the same manner. Award yourself 1 point for each shot that travels through the cones. Shoot back and forth with your classmate until you have each taken 40 shots—20 instep drive shots and 20 swerving shots. All shots should be taken from a distance of 20 yards or more from the goal. Alternate shooting with left and right feet.

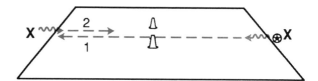

Success Goals =

15 of 20 possible points with instep drive shot

15 of 20 possible points with swerving shot

Your Score =

(#) _____ instep drive shot points

(#) _____ swerving shot points

4. Volley Shots to Partner

Stand facing a classmate 5 yards away. Drop a ball from your hands and volley it out of the air to your classmate's chest. Your classmate catches the ball and returns it to you in the same manner. Take 10 full volley shots, 10 half volleys, and 10 side volley shots. Alternate shooting with your left and right feet. Award yourself 1 point for each shot kicked directly at your classmate so he or she can catch it.

Success Goals =

8 of 10 possible points with full volley

7 of 10 possible points with half volley

6 of 10 possible points with side volley

Your Score =

(#) _____ full volley points

(#) _____ half volley points

(#) _____ side volley points

5. *Toss and Volley to Goal*

Position yourself with a ball 20 yards front and center of a regulation goal. Do not use a goalkeeper. Toss the ball up in the air so it drops a couple of yards from you. Move to the ball and volley it toward the goal after it has bounced once. Repeat with the half volley and side volley shots. Take 10 shots with each type of volley (5 with each foot). Award yourself 1 point for each shot that enters the goal.

Success Goals =

7 of 10 possible points with full volley

6 of 10 possible points with half volley

5 of 10 possible points with side volley

Your Score =

(#) _____ full volley points

(#) _____ half volley points

(#) _____ side volley points

6. *Control and Shoot*

Position yourself 20 yards front and center of a regulation goal while a classmate is positioned in the flank area of the field. Have the classmate serve balls for you to control and shoot on goal. Try to control each ball with your first touch and shoot to score with your second touch. Receive and shoot 30 serves using the shooting technique of your choice. You are free to shoot with either foot; make the appropriate choice for each situation. Award yourself 1 point for each ball that you control and shoot into the goal using only two touches. Do not use a goalkeeper.

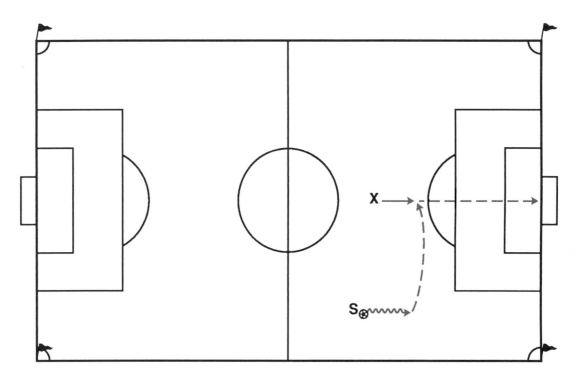

Success Goal = 15 of 30 possible points

Your Score = (#) _____ points

7. *Pressure Shooting in the Penalty Area*

This drill adds the element of physical fatigue to the shooting exercise. Position a server 25 yards from the goal with 10 soccer balls. You stand 2 yards from the server with your back to the goal. A goalkeeper is positioned in the goal. The server rolls or tosses a ball 2 or 3 yards past you. Quickly turn and sprint to the ball, shoot to score, and then sprint back to your original spot. The server immediately

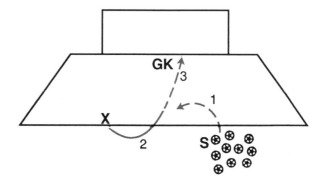

rolls a second ball past you. Again you turn, sprint to the ball, and shoot to score. You must shoot each ball without stopping or controlling it. Use the appropriate shooting technique for each situation. The server should alternate serving balls to your left and right feet. Continue the drill until you have taken 10 shots, then switch roles with the server. Award yourself 2 points for each goal scored and 1 point for each shot on goal that is saved by the goalkeeper.

Success Goal = 15 of 20 possible points

Your Score = (#) _____ points

8. *Game With a Central Goal*

Select six classmates to participate with you in this exercise. Designate one player as the neutral goalkeeper; organize the remaining players, including you, into two teams of three players each. Play in an area of approximately 30 by 30 yards. Position two cones or flags in the center of the area to form a goal 8 yards wide. The neutral goalkeeper is positioned between the goalposts and attempts to save all shots. Your team begins with possession of the ball; the opponents must defend. The objective is to score by kicking the ball through the central goal. Goals can be scored from either side of the central goal; the goalkeeper must readjust his or her position depending on the location of the ball. A goal is scored when the ball passes through the goal below the height of the goalkeeper. A ball that goes out of the playing area is returned with a throw-in. If the defending team gains possession of the ball it immediately switches to the attack and tries to score. If the goalkeeper makes a save he or she throws the ball away from the goal area but within the playing area. Both teams then compete for possession as play continues. Play the game for 15 minutes.

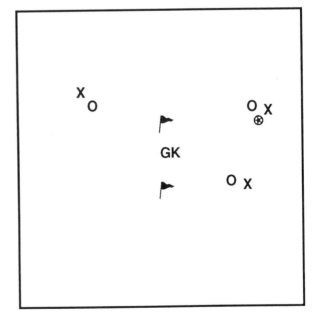

Success Goal = your team scores more goals than opponent

Your Score =

(#) _____ your goals scored

(#) _____ opponent's goals scored

9. Goal Scoring Derby

Select five classmates to participate with you in this exercise. Designate one classmate as the goalkeeper and one as the server, and divide the remaining classmates, including you, into two teams of two players each. Both teams position themselves in an 18-by-44-yard penalty area on a regulation soccer field. The goalkeeper is positioned in the goal and the server is at the top of the penalty area with 8 to 10 soccer balls. The exercise begins as the server tosses a ball into the penalty area. Both teams vie for possession; the team that wins the ball attempts to score while the other team defends. If a defending player steals the ball, his or her team immediately attacks and tries to score in the common goal. The goalkeeper is neutral and attempts to save all shots. After a goal is scored, the goalkeeper makes a save, or the ball is kicked out of the penalty area, the server tosses another ball into the playing area. Continue the drill until the supply of soccer balls has been depleted. The team scoring the most goals wins the competition. Designate a new goalkeeper and server, reorganize the teams, and repeat the exercise. Play the game a sufficient number of times so that all players get an opportunity to play two-against-two in the penalty area.

Success Goal = your team scores more goals than opponent

Your Score =

(#) _____ your goals scored

(#) _____ opponent's goals scored

Shooting Skills
Keys to Success Checklists

Ask a trained observer—your teacher, your coach, or a classmate—to critically analyze your shooting skills. The observer should focus attention on specific aspects of performance that are common to all types of shots. The position of your balance foot, the position of your kicking foot, the position of the knee of your kicking leg in relation to the ball, and the position of your head are all important determinants of shooting success. The observer can use the checklists in Figures 7.1 to 7.3 to evaluate your performance and provide corrective feedback.

Step 8 Goalkeeping

To this point you have learned the basic skills used by field players. Now you will learn an entirely different set of skills, those used by the goalkeeper. The goalkeeper is the one true specialist on the soccer team. He or she is the only player allowed to use the hands to receive and control the ball. The goalkeeper position is very demanding, both physically and mentally, and requires a special type of athlete.

To play as a goalkeeper you must master a set of skills completely different from those used by field players. You must be able to receive and control all types of shots directed at your goal. Sometimes you have to dive to save shots to your side. You are also responsible for initiating your team's attack after you make a save. Basic goalkeeping skills include the proper stance (the ready position); methods of receiving low, medium, chest-high, and high balls; methods of diving; and methods of distributing the ball by rolling, throwing, or punting it to teammates. All players should have a basic understanding of goalkeeping skills in case they are called on to play in the goal.

WHY ARE GOALKEEPING SKILLS IMPORTANT?

The goalkeeper is assigned the task of protecting a goal that is 8 feet high and 24 feet wide and represents the final barrier that opponents must bypass to score. If the goalkeeper doesn't successfully stop shots, the result is a score for the opponents.

HOW TO POSITION YOURSELF IN THE BASIC GOALKEEPER STANCE

The keeper should assume the basic stance, commonly called the *ready position*, whenever an opponent has possession of the ball within shooting distance of the goal. Square your shoulders with the ball and position your feet approximately shoulder-width apart. Point your toes in the direction of the ball. Keep your head and upper body erect with knees flexed. Center your body weight forward over the balls of your feet so your heels rise slightly off the ground. Carry your hands at approximately waist level with palms forward and fingers pointing up. Focus your vision on the ball (see Figure 8.1).

Figure 8.1 Keys to Success:
The Goalkeeper Stance

**Preparation
Phase**

1. Focus vision on ball ____

2. Anticipate shot ____

**Execution
Phase**

1. Square shoulders with ball ____
2. Feet shoulder-width apart ____
3. Toes pointing toward ball ____
4. Upper body erect ____
5. Knees flexed ____
6. Weight forward over balls of feet ____
7. Heels off ground ____
8. Hands at waist level ____
9. Palms forward ____
10. Fingers pointed up ____
11. Focus vision on ball ____

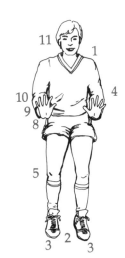

**Follow-Through
Phase**

1. React to shot ____

2. Receive and control ball ____

Detecting Errors
in the Basic Goalkeeper Stance

Assume the ready position whenever the ball is within shooting range of your goal. This ensures that your concentration is focused on the ball and also prepares you to quickly move in any direction to make the save. Common errors that occur with the basic goalkeeper stance are listed here along with suggested corrections.

ERROR

CORRECTION

1. You find it difficult to quickly react to a shot.

1. You are probably failing to center your weight forward over the balls of your feet. Do not lean back. Your heels should be slightly elevated off the ground when you are in the ready position.

HOW TO RECEIVE A BALL ROLLING DIRECTLY AT THE GOALKEEPER

From the ready position move quickly to position your body between the ball and the goal. Remain in a standing position with your feet only a few inches apart. Keep your legs straight and bend forward at the waist as the ball arrives. Point your fingers downward with your palms facing forward and slightly cupped. Do not catch the ball on your palms. Let the ball roll up onto your wrists and forearms, then return to an upright position with the ball clutched against your chest (see Figure 8.2a-d).

HOW TO RECEIVE A BALL ROLLING TO THE SIDE OF THE GOALKEEPER

Sometimes you will not have time to position your body between the ball and the goal. This type of shot, sometimes called the *tweener*, is just far enough away to make a standing save impossible but not so far as to require a diving save. Move laterally across the goal to intercept the oncoming ball. Extend your lead foot in the direction you are moving and kneel on the trailing leg. Position the trailing leg parallel to the goal line. Allow only a small space between your lead foot and the knee of the trailing leg so the ball can't skid through your legs. From this position bend your upper body forward with shoulders square to the ball. Let the ball roll up onto your wrists and forearms and then clutch it to your chest (see Figure 8.2e-i).

Figure 8.2 Keys to Success:
Receiving
Rolling Balls

**Preparation
Phase**

Directly At

To the Side

a

e

f

g

1. Position yourself be-
   tween ball and goal ____
2. Upright posture ____
3. Feet a few inches
   apart ____
4. Focus vision on ball ____

1. Move laterally across
   goal ____
2. Extend lead foot ____
3. Kneel on trailing
   leg ____
4. Trailing leg parallel to
   goal line ____
5. Focus vision on ball ____

Execution
Phase

Directly At

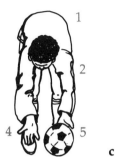

b   c

To the Side

h

1. Bend forward at waist _____
2. Legs straight _____
3. Fingertips touching ground _____
4. Palms forward and cupped _____
5. Contact ball on palms _____
6. Let ball roll onto wrists and forearms _____

1. Bend forward _____
2. Shoulders square to ball _____
3. Palms forward and fingers pointed down _____
4. Let ball roll onto wrists and forearms _____

Follow-Through
Phase

Directly At

d

To the Side

_____ 1. Clutch ball against chest with forearms _____
_____ 2. Return to standing position _____
_____ 3. Distribute ball _____

i

Detecting Errors
in Receiving Rolling Balls

Inexperienced goalkeepers commonly make the following errors. You can avoid these mistakes by using the correct technique to collect balls rolling directly at you or to your side.

ERROR    **CORRECTION**

ERROR	CORRECTION
1. The ball rolls through your hands, between your legs, and into the goal.	1. Always position your body behind the ball as you collect it. Your legs should be only a few inches apart. If the ball happens to slip between your hands it will rebound off your legs rather than go past you.
2. You fail to hold the ball and it bounces off your hands into the area in front of the goal.	2. This usually occurs when you try to catch a hard, low shot with your hands. Remember, do not catch a low rolling ball with your hands. Let the ball roll up onto your wrists and forearms, then return to an upright position and clutch the ball to your chest.

HOW TO RECEIVE MEDIUM-HEIGHT BALLS

A medium-height ball is one arriving between the ankles and the waist. Position your body in line with the ball with your legs straight and your feet a few inches apart. As the ball arrives bend your upper body forward. Extend your arms down with palms forward. As with rolling balls, do not attempt to catch the ball in the palms of your hands. Allow the ball to contact your wrists and forearms before you secure it against your body. Jump slightly backward as you receive the ball to absorb the impact. The harder the shot, the more cushion you must provide so the ball doesn't bounce away from you (see Figure 8.3a-d).

HOW TO RECEIVE CHEST-HIGH BALLS

Position your body in line and square your shoulders with the oncoming ball. Your palms should face forward with fingers pointed toward the oncoming ball. Put your hands in what is generally referred to as the *W (window) position* with the fingers spread and thumbs almost touching. Your arms should be partially extended and flexed at the elbow. In contrast to the techniques used to field low shots, you should actually try to catch a chest-high shot in your hands.

Always follow an important principle of goalkeeping when receiving a chest-high ball—the HEH, or ''hands-eyes-head,'' principle. Whenever possible position your hands, eyes, and head in line with the ball as you receive it. Follow the flight of the ball into your hands by looking through the window formed by your thumbs and index fingers. Receive the ball on your fingertips. Cushion the impact of the shot by withdrawing your arms toward your body, then secure the ball to your chest (see Figure 8.3e-i).

HOW TO RECEIVE HIGH LOFTED BALLS

A high lofted ball crossed from the flank areas can pose problems for a goalkeeper. Receiving and controlling a high lofted ball demands correct technique, proper balance, precise timing, and good judgment. Face the ball as it approaches the goal area. Your objective is to catch the ball at the highest point possible by jumping up and extending your arms overhead. The proper jumping technique is the one-leg takeoff. It is essential that you leap off the correct foot. The outside leg (the one toward the field) should be thrust upward with knee flexed, whereas the leg closest to the goal remains straight and serves as the balance leg. Thrust your arms and leg up in one fluid movement to generate the greatest momentum. Keep your hands in the W position and follow the HEH principle discussed earlier. Watch the ball until the moment it contacts your hands, then secure it to your chest (see Figure 8.3j-m).

Figure 8.3 Keys to Success: Receiving Aerial Balls

Preparation Phase

Medium Height

1. Position yourself in line with ball ____
2. Upright posture with legs slightly apart ____
3. Arms extended downward ____
4. Fingers pointed down and palms forward ____
5. Vision focused on ball ____

Chest High

1. Align body with ball ____
2. Square shoulders with ball ____
3. Feet shoulder-width apart ____
4. Hands in W position at chest level ____
5. Palms forward ____
6. Fingers pointed toward ball ____
7. Vision focused on ball ____

High Lofted

1. Face oncoming ball ____
2. Shoulders square ____
3. Move toward ball ____
4. Vision focused on ball ____

Execution
Phase

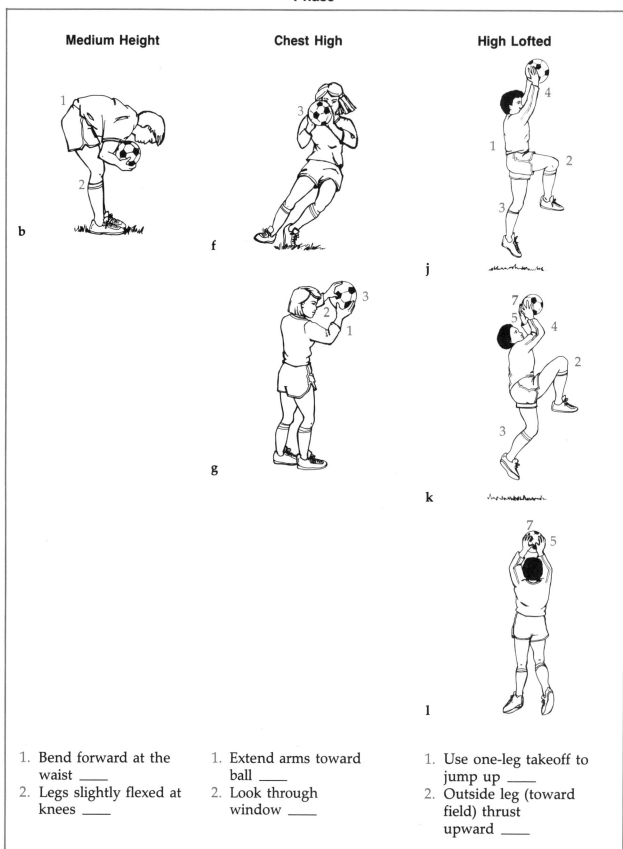

Medium Height

b

Chest High

f

g

High Lofted

j

k

l

1. Bend forward at the
   waist ____
2. Legs slightly flexed at
   knees ____

1. Extend arms toward
   ball ____
2. Look through
   window ____

1. Use one-leg takeoff to
   jump up ____
2. Outside leg (toward
   field) thrust
   upward ____

Medium Height	**Chest High**	**High Lofted**
3. Contact ball on wrists and forearms _____ 4. Allow ball to roll up onto forearms _____	3. Receive ball on fingertips _____	3. Inside leg remains straight _____ 4. Arms thrust upward _____ 5. Hands in W position _____ 6. Head behind hands (HEH principle) _____ 7. Receive ball on fingers and palms _____

Follow-Through
Phase

Medium Height	**Chest High**	**High Lofted**
 c  d	 h  i	 m
1. Jump slightly backward to cushion shot _____ 2. Clutch ball with fore-arms against chest _____ 3. Distribute ball _____	1. Withdraw arms _____ 2. Secure ball to chest _____ 3. Distribute ball _____	1. Withdraw arms and hands _____ 2. Descend to ground _____ 3. Secure ball to chest _____ 4. Distribute ball _____

Detecting Errors in Receiving Aerial Balls

The most common errors players make when receiving balls out of the air are listed here along with suggestions for correcting them.

ERROR    **CORRECTION**

Receiving a Medium-Height Ball

1. You fail to control the ball.

2. The ball rebounds off your arms and out of your control.

1. Do not attempt to catch the ball in your hands. Receive the ball on your wrists and forearms, then clutch it to your chest.

2. Jump back a few inches as the ball contacts your arms to absorb the impact.

Receiving a Chest-High Ball

1. The ball slips through your hands as you receive it.

1. Proper position of your hands behind the ball will prevent the shot from slipping between your hands. Position your hands to form a window (W position). Thumbs and forefingers should almost touch behind the ball as you receive it.

Receiving a High Lofted Ball

1. You fail to generate sufficient height on your jump.

2. You jump too early and the ball goes over your head.

1. Thrust your arms and takeoff leg upward in one fluid motion to generate maximum height on your jump.

2. Face the ball, judge its trajectory, and then move toward the ball as you prepare to jump. Wait until the last possible moment, then use a one-leg takeoff to leap up and receive the ball at the highest point of your jump.

HOW TO DIVE TO SAVE SHOTS

The most difficult save for the goalkeeper is the low, hard shot to his or her side. The initial diving movement begins from the ready position. You must coordinate the movement of your legs and upper body to vault to the spot where you can intercept the ball. Push off with the foot nearest the ball—for example, push off with your right foot when diving to your right. Your opposite leg and arm follow to generate additional momentum in the direction of your dive. Extend your arms and hands toward the ball. With the correct diving technique you will contact the ground on your side. Do not dive on your stomach; if you do, your back may be exposed to an overly aggressive opponent and you may be injured. Attempt to catch the ball and pin it to the ground by placing one hand behind the ball and one on top of it. If you are unsure you can catch the ball, then deflect it wide of the goal. Use the palm of your lower hand to deflect the shot (see Figure 8.4).

Figure 8.4 Keys to Success: *Diving*

Preparation Phase

1. Assume ready position ___
2. Face ball ___
3. Vision focused on ball ___

a

Execution Phase

1. Step in direction of dive ___
2. Push off with foot nearest ball ___
3. Opposite leg and arm follow ___
4. Dive on your side ___
5. Extend arms and hands toward ball ___
6. Use HEH principle if possible ___
7. Catch ball in hands ___

b

c

**Follow-Through
Phase**

1. Pin ball to ground ____
2. Secure ball to chest ____
3. Stand up ____

4. Distribute ball to teammate ____

Detecting Errors in Diving

Diving is a difficult skill that requires much practice. Common errors players make when diving to save shots are listed here along with suggested corrections.

ERROR ⊘

CORRECTION

1. You dive on your stomach instead of your side.

2. You try to catch a ball that is out of your reach and fail to hold it.

1. Remember to push off the foot nearest to the ball, vault sideways, and land on your side.

2. If you are not sure that you can catch and hold the ball, then deflect the ball wide of the goal using the open palm of your lower hand.

HOW TO DISTRIBUTE THE BALL BY ROLLING

Rolling, or *bowling,* the ball is an effective means of distributing the ball over distances of 15 to 20 yards. The motion looks very similar to that used in bowling. Cup the ball in the palm of your hand, step toward the target, and release the ball with a bowling-type motion. Release the ball at ground level to avoid bouncing (see Figure 8.5a-b).

HOW TO DISTRIBUTE THE BALL BY THROWING

Two techniques are commonly used to throw the ball. The *baseball throw* is used to toss the ball over distances of 20 to 30 yards. As the name implies, the ball is released with a motion similar to that used in throwing a baseball. Hold the ball in the palm of your hand, step toward the target, and use a three-quarter or overhand motion to release the ball. Snap your wrist toward the target to add velocity to the throw (Figure 8.6a-b).

The second method is called the *javelin throw* and is used to toss the ball over long distances. Curl your hand around the ball, encasing it with your fingers, palm, and wrist. Extend your throwing arm back and keep it straight. Arch your body backward. At this point you should be holding the ball at approximately knee level. Step toward the target and snap your upper body forward from the waist. The throwing motion of your arm begins at knee level and moves upward behind your back. The follow-through ends with a whiplike motion of your throwing arm above your head. The point of release can vary depending on the desired trajectory of the toss. The sooner you release the ball along your throwing arc, the higher the trajectory. The ball will travel parallel to the ground if you release it near the completion of your throwing motion (see Figure 8.6c-d).

HOW TO DISTRIBUTE THE BALL BY PUNTING

Punting is also an effective means of distributing the ball to teammates. Although it is not as accurate as throwing, you can usually distribute the ball over greater distances by kicking it. Stand erect and face your target. Hold the ball in the palm of the hand opposite your kicking foot and extend that arm forward so the ball is at approximately waist level. Step forward with the nonkicking foot, release the ball, and then punt the ball using the instep surface of your kicking foot. Keep your head steady and your vision focused on the ball at the moment of contact. A complete follow-through motion of the kicking leg adds height and distance to the punt (see Figure 8.7a-b).

Figure 8.5 *Keys to Success: Distribution by Rolling the Ball*

Preparation Phase

1. Face your target ____
2. Cup ball in palm of hand ____

3. Step toward target ____

Execution Phase

1. Bend forward at waist ____
2. Draw back arm and ball ____
3. Release ball with bowling-type motion ____
4. Vision focused on target ____

a

**Follow-Through
Phase**

1. Follow through with
   throwing hand ____
2. Resume erect
   posture ____

b

Figure 8.6 Keys to Success:
***Distribution
by Throwing***

**Preparation
Phase**

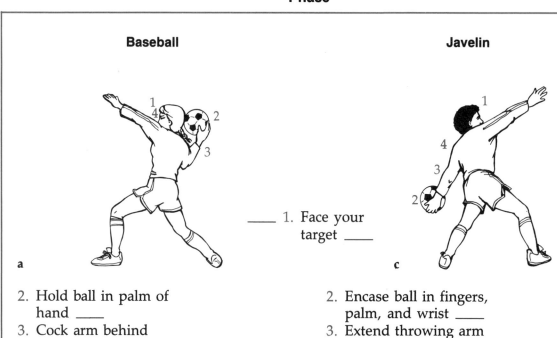

Baseball

Javelin

a

c

____ 1. Face your
     target ____

2. Hold ball in palm of
   hand ____
3. Cock arm behind
   ear ____
4. Vision focused on
   target ____

2. Encase ball in fingers,
   palm, and wrist ____
3. Extend throwing arm
   backward ____
4. Arch upper body
   backward ____

Execution
Phase

Baseball   **Javelin**

b

d

_____ 1. Step toward
target _____

2. Three-quarter or over-
hand motion _____
3. Snap wrist toward
target _____
4. Release ball _____

2. Whiplike motion of
throwing arm toward
target _____
3. Release ball _____

Follow-Through
Phase

Baseball   **Javelin**

_____ 1. Complete follow-
through of
throwing arm _____

Figure 8.7 Keys to Success: Distribution by Punting

Preparation Phase

1. Stand erect ____
2. Face your target ____
3. Extend arms forward ____
4. Hold ball in palm of hand opposite kicking foot ____

5. Ball at waist level ____
6. Head steady with vision focused on ball ____

Execution Phase

1. Step forward with nonkicking foot ____
2. Begin forward movement of kicking leg ____
3. Extend kicking foot ____
4. Kicking foot firm ____
5. Release ball from hand ____
6. Contact ball on instep ____
7. Nonkicking foot leaves ground ____
8. Vision focused on ball ____

Follow-Through Phase

1. Kicking leg to chest level or higher ____

2. Descend to ground ____

Detecting Errors in Distribution

Correct body mechanics will improve the accuracy as well as the distance of your throws and punts. Common distribution errors are listed here along with suggested corrections.

ERROR   **CORRECTION**

Throwing the Ball

1. Your throw lacks accuracy.

2. Your throw lacks distance.

1. Face your target, step toward the target, and use a complete follow-through motion.

2. When using the baseball throw snap your wrist toward the target as you release the ball. When using the javelin throw fully extend your throwing arm backward, then use a whiplike motion of the throwing arm to propel the ball toward the intended target.

Punting the Ball

1. You pull your punt to the right or left of the target.

2. Your punt lacks sufficient height.

3. Your punt lacks sufficient distance.

1. Face forward with shoulders square to the target as you prepare to punt the ball.

2. This occurs usually because you release the ball from your hand too soon and as a result contact it too low to the ground. Hold the ball at approximately waist level and release it just before your foot contacts the ball.

3. Lack of distance is usually due to poor follow-through motion of the kicking leg. Kick through the point of contact with the ball. Your kicking foot should rise to chest level or higher on the follow-through.

Goalkeeping Drills

1. Bounce and Catch

Hold a ball with both hands at approximately chest level. Bounce the ball hard off the ground and receive it with the W catch before it rises above waist level. Repeat 40 times.

Success Goal = 36 of 40 bounces caught

Your Score = (#) _____ balls caught

2. Jump and Catch

While jogging toss a ball high in the air, jump up, and catch the ball at the highest point of your jump. Repeat 30 times.

Success Goal = 25 of 30 tosses caught at highest point of jump

Your Score = (#) _____ tosses caught at highest point of jump

3. Toss and Catch

Select a classmate to participate with you in this exercise. Face your classmate at a distance of 5 yards. Toss the ball to the right or left of your classmate's chest. He or she must catch the ball using the W catch and the HEH (hands-eyes-head) principle. Your classmate then tosses the ball and you must catch it in the same manner. Attempt to catch 40 tosses each.

Success Goal = 35 of 40 tosses caught and held

Your Score = (#) _____ tosses caught and held

4. Volley and Catch

Select a classmate to participate with you in this exercise. Face your classmate at a distance of 8 to 10 yards. Volley a ball back and forth to each other. Catch each volley shot using the W hand position and the HEH principle. Kick and receive 40 volleys each.

Success Goal = 32 of 40 volleys caught and held

Your Score = (#) _____ volleys caught and held

5. Shuffle and Catch

Select three classmates to participate with you in this exercise. The classmates, each with a ball, position themselves as servers along the 6-yard line in front of the goal. You are positioned near one of the goalposts facing the servers. Slowly shuffle across the front of the goal. Server number 1 serves a rolling ball at you that you collect and return. Continue to shuffle as server 2 serves a medium-height ball at you. Receive the ball, return it to the server, and continue to shuffle across the goal. Server 3 then serves you a chest-high ball. Receive it and return it to the server, then walk back to the original starting point. Repeat 10 times for a total of 30 balls received.

   You can also use a variation of this exercise. Organize in the same manner except with your back toward the server as you shuffle across the goal. On the server's command you must spin and receive either a low, medium, or chest-high ball—the servers are permitted to vary the type of service. Complete 10 circuits for a total of 30 tosses.

Success Goal = 26 of 30 serves received and controlled

Your Score = (#) _____ balls received and controlled

6. Kneeling Save to Side

Face a classmate 10 yards away. Serve a rolling ball to his or her left. Your classmate must move to the ball, receive it, and then serve a rolling ball to your right. Move to the ball, receive it, and serve a rolling ball to your classmate's right. He or she moves laterally to receive it, then rolls a ball to your left. Continue the sequence until you have each received 10 rolling balls to each side for a total of 20 balls.

Success Goals =

   8 of 10 successfully fielded balls to your right
   8 of 10 successfully fielded balls to your left

Your Score =

   (#) _____ of 10 balls fielded to right
   (#) _____ of 10 balls fielded to left

7. Post to Post

Select two classmates to participate as servers with you in this exercise. Position a server in line with each goalpost, 10 yards out from the goal line. Stand near the right goalpost facing the servers. The server in front of you (server 1) rolls a ball to your left, toward the center of the goal. Move to your left, receive the rolling ball, and return it to server 2. Continue to shuffle across the goal mouth. When you reach the opposite post, server 2 rolls the ball to your right, toward the center of the goal. Move to the ball, receive it using the proper technique, and return the ball to server 1. Continue back and forth from post to post until you have received 20 rolling balls.

Success Goal = 18 of 20 balls received without error

Your Score = (#) _____ of 20 balls received without error

8. Four-Player Drill

Select three classmates to participate as servers in this drill. The servers, each with a ball, are positioned in a circle around you at a distance of 15 yards. Each server in turn tosses a high ball toward you. Move toward the ball, leap up using the correct takeoff leg, and catch the ball at the highest possible point of your jump. Receive 30 tosses.

Success Goal = 25 of 30 tosses received at highest point

Your Score = (#) _____ of 30 tosses received at highest point

9. Diving From Knees

Assume a kneeling position with a ball placed to each side within your reach. Practice diving to your left, then right, left, and so forth to save the stationary ball. Emphasize the correct technique of landing on your side while placing one hand behind the ball and one on top of it to pin it to the ground. Repeat 20 times.

Success Goal = 18 of 20 correct dives to stationary ball

Your Score = (#) _____ correct dives

10. Diving From Squat Position

Move the balls farther from you. Repeat the previous drill beginning your dive from a squatting position. Make 20 dives.

Success Goal = 16 of 20 correct dives

Your Score = (#) _____ correct dives

11. Standing Dive

Select a classmate to participate as a server in this exercise. Assume the ready position and face your classmate at a distance of 10 yards. The classmate serves balls to your side at varying speeds. Dive and save each ball, then return it to the server. Repeat 10 times to each side.

Success Goal = 7 of 10 balls saved to each side

Your Score =

    (#) _____ of 10 balls saved to your right

    (#) _____ of 10 balls saved to your left

12. Partner Throw

Select a classmate to participate with you in this exercise. Practice distributing the ball to each other over varying distances:

- Rolling balls—15 yards apart
- Baseball throw—30 yards apart
- Javelin throw—45 yards apart

A throw is considered accurate if your classmate does not have to move more than three steps in any direction to receive the ball. Do 20 repetitions of each type of throw.

Success Goals =

    18 of 20 accurate rolling balls

    16 of 20 accurate baseball throws

    14 of 20 accurate javelin throws

Your Score =

    (#) _____ accurate rolling balls

    (#) _____ accurate baseball throws

    (#) _____ accurate javelin throws

13. Punt Into Net

Stand 3 yards in front of a regulation goal with a goal net. Practice punting the ball into the net from directly in front of the goal. Repeat 30 times.

Success Goal = 30 of 30 punts kicked straight upward into the goal net

Your Score = (#) _____ punts kicked straight upward into the goal net

14. Punt Into Circle

Stand on the penalty spot 12 yards in front of the goal. Attempt to punt the ball so it lands within the center circle of the field. Award yourself 2 points for each punt that lands within the circle on the fly and 1 point for each ball that bounces into the circle on one hop. Attempt 20 punts.

Success Goal = 25 of 40 possible points

Your Score = (#) _____ points

Goalkeeping
Keys to Success Checklists

Ask your teacher, your coach, or a classmate to observe you in a goalkeeping situation. The observer should pay particular attention to your consistent ability to stop shots. He or she can use the checklists in Figures 8.1 to 8.7 to evaluate your performance and provide corrective feedback.

Step 9   Small Group Strategies in Attack

The skills and tactics discussed thus far have dealt primarily with individual play. In the final analysis, however, soccer is a team game. Much like the pieces of a puzzle, individual players must fit together in the correct combinations to complete the picture. Team objectives cannot be achieved unless individual players combine their efforts toward a common goal. Two small group strategies are essential for successful attacking play—the *give and go pass* and *support*.

WHY ARE SMALL GROUP STRATEGIES IN ATTACK IMPORTANT?

Successful attacking soccer consists of much more than brilliant individual play. It also requires teamwork within groups of two or more players. A key to success is getting more attacking players than defending players in the vicinity of the ball. Once that has been accomplished, these players must then work together to beat opposing players and advance with the ball.

HOW TO EXECUTE THE GIVE AND GO PASS

The basic foundation for group attacking tactics is the two-versus-one situation—two attackers versus one defender. The most effective method of beating a single defender in a two-versus-one situation is the give and go, or wall, pass. The basic concept is quite simple. The player with the ball dribbles at and commits the defending player to him or her, then passes the ball to a nearby teammate before sprinting forward to collect a return pass. Executing the give and go pass is not quite as easy as it sounds, however. The player with possession of the ball as well as his or her teammate, referred to as the support player, must both fulfill specific responsibilities. Precise skill execution, correct timing, and a conceptual understanding of the tactics involved are all important elements needed for the successful give and go pass.

When you have possession of the ball in a two-versus-one situation, you should perform the following steps in the order listed.

1. *Take on the defender*. Immediately dribble at the defending player as soon as you realize that a two-versus-one situation exists.
2. *Commit the defender*. Draw the defending player toward you as he or she prepares to tackle.
3. *Pass the ball*. Release your pass as the defender closes to tackle. Use the outside surface of your instep to pass the ball to the lead foot of your teammate.
4. *Sprint into space*. Sprint forward past the defending player after passing the ball.
5. *Collect the return pass*. Receive the return pass from your teammate (see Figure 9.1a).

When you are the support player you must perform the following steps.

1. *Move toward the ball*. Quickly move to a position near the ball. Position yourself 3 to 4 yards to the side of the defending player at an angle of approximately 45 degrees from the player with the ball.
2. *Serve as the wall*. Use an open stance with your body turned toward the teammate with possession of the ball. Your lead foot serves as the wall off which the ball is passed. Keep your passing foot firmly positioned as the ball rebounds off the inside surface of your foot.
3. *Use a one-touch pass into space*. Direct the moving ball into the space behind the defender by passing the ball without stopping it first. This is known as passing the ball with the first touch.

4. *Support your teammate.* Sprint forward to support your teammate after passing the ball (see Figure 9.1b).

HOW TO EXECUTE SUPPORT IN ATTACK

It is also essential that teammates provide the player who has the ball with several passing options. The more options there are available, the less likely it is that defending players will be able to anticipate what the player with the ball is going to do. This can be accomplished through the small group strategy of support in attack—the movement of players to positions near the teammate with the ball.

Providing adequate support for the player who has the ball involves several factors, including (a) the number of support players, (b) the angle of support, and (c) the distance of support.

Number of Support Players

The number of support players in the vicinity of the ball is of critical importance. Too few support players limit passing options for the player with the ball. Too many support players can also be a disadvantage because they will attract additional defending players around the ball, thus reducing the available space. As a general guideline, the player with the ball should have a minimum of two and a maximum of three teammates in close support positions. Support players generally position themselves to the side of and behind the player with the ball.

Angle of Support

Two support players should position themselves to form a wide angle with the player who has the ball. If you can imagine two lines drawn from the ball, one to each supporting player, the angle formed by these two lines should be 90 degrees or greater (Figure 9.2).

A defending player challenging for the ball cannot possibly cover both support players if they are positioned in a wide angle of support but may be able to if they are positioned in a narrow angle of support. If a third support player is present, he or she should be positioned behind the player with the ball.

Distance of Support

Base your distance decision on the position of defending player(s), and the area of the field. As a general rule, position yourself within 3 to 5 yards of the ball if a defending player is preparing to challenge for possession. You can support from a greater distance, possibly 8 to 10 yards, if the defending player is not preparing to challenge for possession or if the space around the ball is not crowded with players.

The distance of the support players from the ball should be reduced when the ball is in the opponent's end of the field. The defending team will usually consolidate its players in their defending zone to reduce the space available to the attacking team. In the midfield zone of the field, where space is generally not as restricted, the distance of support players from the ball can be greater (see Figure 9.3).

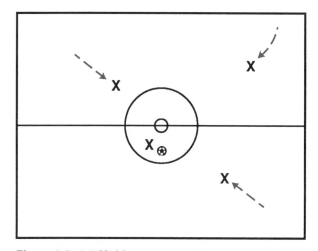

Figure 9.3 Midfield support positions.

Figure 9.1 Keys to Success:
Give and Go Pass

Preparation Phase

Player With Ball

1. Control ball ____
2. Face defending opponent ____

Support Player

1. Move toward teammate with ball ____
2. Position 3 to 4 yards to side of defending player ____
3. Use open stance ____
4. Face teammate with ball ____

Execution Phase

Player With Ball

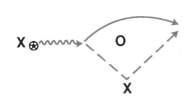

a

1. Dribble at opponent ____
2. Commit opponent to you ____
3. Pass to support player ____
4. Use outside-of-the-foot pass ____
5. Pass ball to lead foot of support player ____

Support Player

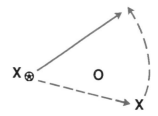

b

1. Extend lead foot ____
2. Keep foot firm ____
3. Contact ball on inside of foot ____
4. One-touch pass behind defender ____

Follow-Through
Phase

Player With Ball

1. Sprint forward ____
2. Receive wall pass behind opponent ____
3. Dribble toward goal ____

Support Player

1. Sprint forward ____
2. Support teammate with ball ____

Figure 9.2 Keys to Success:
Support in Attack

Preparation
Phase

1. Move to position near ball ____
2. Maintain open passing lane to ball ____
3. Position to side of or behind teammate with ball ____
4. Position to form wide angle of support ____
5. Vision focused on ball and defender ____

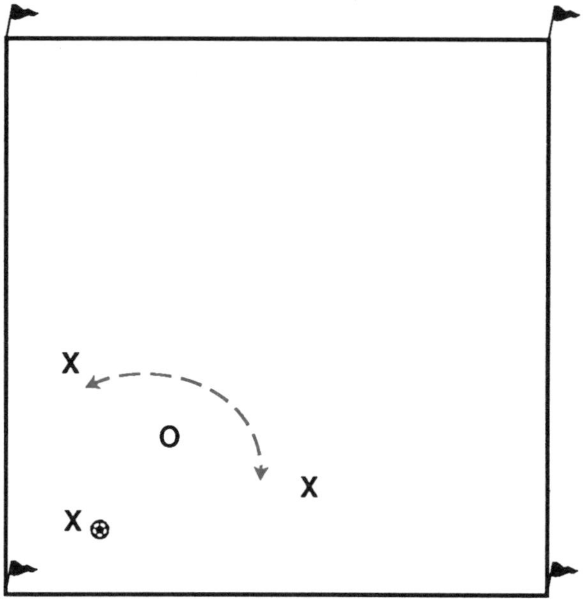

Execution Phase

1. Receive pass from teammate ____
2. Maintain possession ____

3. Turn with ball toward opposing goal if possible ____

Follow-Through Phase

1. Dribble toward goal ____
2. Look for nearby support players ____

3. Pass to support player ____

Detecting Errors in Small Group Attacking Strategies

Errors in small group attacking strategies occur for a variety of reasons because both skill execution and decision making are involved in every situation. A poorly paced or inaccurate pass, improper position of the support player, or failure of the dribbler to commit the defender can result in technical breakdown of the passing combinations. Common errors are listed here along with suggested corrections.

ERROR    **CORRECTION**

Give and Go Pass

1. The defending player does not commit to you.

1. Dribble at speed directly at the defender, forcing him or her to make a decision—either retreat or challenge for possession. If the defending player retreats, try to beat him or her on the dribble and go to goal. If the defender steps forward to tackle the ball, use the give and go pass with a supporting teammate.

ERROR ⊘	CORRECTION
2. You pass the ball to your supporting teammate but he or she cannot execute the give and go pass with you.	2. This can occur for two reasons. First, the support player may be positioned too far away from you. Proper support position is 3 to 4 yards to the side of the defender; support at a greater distance gives the defender time to readjust his or her position to intercept the return pass. The second possible reason is that you fail to sprint forward after passing the ball. Immediately move into the space behind the defender after passing the ball.

Support Play

1. The challenging defender blocks the passing lane between you and the ball.	1. You must position yourself at a wide angle from the ball. Never position yourself behind the challenging defender.
2. Your support position is square with the teammate who has the ball.	2. Support players should position themselves either to the side and ahead of the player with the ball or behind that player. He or she will then have the option of passing the ball forward or passing it back to the trailing support player who can then pass it forward to an open teammate.

Small Group Attacking Drills

1. Playing the Wall

Select a classmate to be a support player. Practice the wall pass with your classmate against an imaginary defender as you jog the length of the field. Pass the ball to the lead foot of the "wall" who then one-touches the ball ahead into space. Award yourself 1 point for each successful pass to the support player's lead foot. Award the support player 1 point for each one-touch pass forward into space. Perform the exercise at half speed. Concentrate on correct timing of the pass and run. Execute 30 wall passes, then switch positions with your classmate.

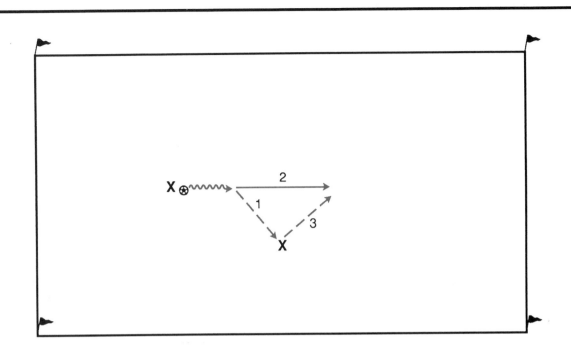

Success Goals =

25 of 30 possible points as player with the ball

25 of 30 possible points as support player

Your Score =

(#) _____ points as player with the ball

(#) _____ points as support player

2. Shadow Drill (3 vs. 0)

Select two classmates to participate with you in this exercise. Use cones or flags to mark off a 10-by-10-yard grid. Stand in one corner of the grid with the ball while your classmates position themselves in adjacent corners of the grid. Pass the ball to one of your classmates while the other runs along a sideline of the grid to a support position in a corner adjacent to the position of the ball. The classmate who received the ball then passes it to another player and the uninvolved player runs to the proper support position (corner of the grid). Continue the exercise as each player passes the ball, receives the ball, or moves to a new support position within the grid. The player with possession of the ball should always have a supporting teammate in each adjacent corner of the grid. Continue the exercise until each player has made 20 supporting runs.

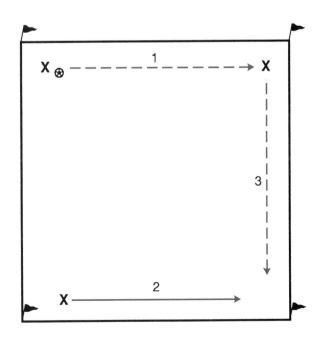

Success Goal = 20 of 20 support runs made to the correct corner of the grid with relation to the position of the ball

Your Score = (#) ____ of 20 correct support runs

3. Two Versus One in the Grid

Select two classmates to participate with you in this exercise. You and a classmate form a team and play against the single defender in a 10-by-10-yard grid. Use dribbling, shielding, and passing skills to maintain possession from the defender. Your team is awarded 2 points each time you and your teammate use a give and go pass to beat the defender within the grid and 1 point each time you combine for five or more consecutive passes without loss of possession. The defender is awarded 1 point each time he or she intercepts a pass or if your team passes the ball outside of the grid area. Play for 10 minutes.

Success Goal = as a team score more points than defender

Your Score =
   (#) ____ your points
   (#) ____ defender's points

4. Keep-Away Game (3 vs. 1)

Select three classmates to participate with you in this exercise. Designate one classmate as a defender while you join with the remaining classmates to form a team. Play within a 10-by-10-yard grid. The objective is for your team of three players to keep the ball away from the defender within the boundaries of the grid. Your team is awarded 1 point for each time you and your teammates make 10 or more consecutive passes without losing possession to the defender. Play for 5 minutes, then switch defenders.

Success Goal = 5 or more points scored as a team in 5 minutes

Your Score = (#) ____ points

5. Two Versus One to the Line

Select two classmates to participate with you in this exercise. Team up with one player and position yourselves 25 yards from the endline of the field. The third player stands facing you on the endline with a ball. He or she passes the ball to you and immediately sprints forward to defend. You receive the ball and then attempt to take on and beat the defender using a give and go pass with your teammate. Your team is awarded 1 point if you beat the defender to the endline using the give and go pass. Repeat 10 times, then switch defenders.

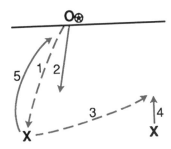

Success Goal = 7 of a possible 10 points scored as a team

Your Score = (#) _____ points

6. Two Versus One Plus One

Select three classmates to participate with you in this exercise. Organize two teams of two players each. Mark off a playing area of 20 by 30 yards with a goal 4 yards wide at the center of each endline. Each team defends its goal and tries to score in the opponent's goal. Your team begins the game with possession of the ball. The rules of play are as follows. The team that has the ball tries to score by passing the ball through the opponent's goal. The defending team tries to prevent scores by positioning one player as a goalkeeper and one as a defender. If the defending team steals the ball the goalkeeper moves forward out of the goal and joins his or her teammate, and both players attack and attempt to score in the opposing goal. The team that lost possession must defend—one player sprints back to play as the goalkeeper while his or her teammate plays as the defender. Play is continuous as teams attack with two players and defend with one player and a goalkeeper. One point is awarded to a team for each give and go pass that beats a defender; an additional 1 point is awarded for each goal scored. Play for 15 minutes and keep track of points scored.

Success Goal = score more points than opponent

Your Score =

  (#) _____ your points
  (#) _____ opponent's points

7. Three Versus One to Goal

Select three classmates to participate with you in this exercise. Play on one half of a regulation field or in a large gymnasium. Position a regulation-size goal on the endline of the playing area. You and two teammates position yourselves 30 yards from the goal with a ball. The remaining classmate is positioned as a defender between your team and the goal. The objective of the exercise is for your team to score against the single defender who tries to gain possession of the ball. After each score your team restarts the game from the 30-yard line.

Your team is awarded 1 point for each goal scored; the defender is awarded 2 points each time he or she gains possession of the ball. Do not use a goalkeeper. Play for 10 minutes and keep track of scores.

Success Goal = score more points than defender

Your Score =

(#) ____ your points

(#) ____ defender's points

Small Group Attacking Strategies Keys to Success Checklists

Ask your teacher, your coach, or a classmate to observe you in a two-versus-one and a three-versus-one tactical situation. Alternate playing as the player with the ball and as the support player. The observer can use the checklists in Figures 9.1 and 9.2 to evaluate your performance and provide corrective feedback.

Step 10 Small Group Strategies in Defense

Defensive and offensive strategies are like different sides of the same coin. The objectives of each are opposite yet connected in the sense that players must always be able to make the transition from one to the other during the course of a game. *Cover* and *balance* are two defensive strategies commonly used in game situations. Successful execution of cover and balance requires teamwork among two or more defending players.

WHY ARE COVER AND BALANCE IN DEFENSE IMPORTANT?

Just as attacking players use small group strategies to create scoring opportunities, defending players must also work together in an attempt to prevent scores. The strategies of defensive cover and balance are designed to achieve that aim.

HOW TO EXECUTE COVER AND BALANCE IN DEFENSE

Defensive cover is quite similar to the attacking strategy of support in that the player challenging for the ball, referred to as the first defender, is supported by one or more teammates. A supporting teammate is usually called the second, or covering, defender. The second defender gets into position behind the first defender so that if the first defender is beaten, he or she can step up to confront the opponent and prevent a penetrating run toward the goal. The second defender is also responsible for preventing the opponents from passing the ball through the space behind the first defender. The covering defender is like the free safety in American football, a player who is free to cover space and help teammates when needed.

Balance in defense is generally provided by one or more players positioned diagonally be-

hind the second defender and commonly referred to as the third defender(s). The third defender is responsible for preventing opposing players from passing the ball diagonally through the defense. Balance in defense is designed to protect the vulnerable space between the last line of defense and the goalkeeper.

The defender nearest the ball (first defender) and his or her covering teammate (second defender) must work in tandem. Each player has specific responsibilities.

Responsibilities of the First Defender

The first defender has the primary responsibility of applying direct pressure to the opponent with possession of the ball. He or she should be positioned goalside of the dribbler in proper defensive posture and attempt to do one of three things: (a) delay the dribbler until defending teammates can recover goalside of the ball, (b) force the dribbler into restricted space near the sideline, or (c) force the dribbler into space where the covering defender can tackle the ball. The first defender should not attempt to tackle the ball until a teammate is in a position to provide cover (see Figure 10.1).

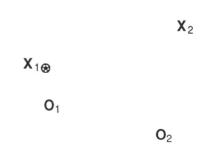

Figure 10.1 Positions of the first and second defenders.

Responsibilities of the Second Defender

The second defender has two primary responsibilities. The first is to cover the space behind and to the side of the first defender. From that position he or she can prevent a penetrating pass through that space and can also step forward to challenge the dribbler if the first defender is beaten. In most situations the second defender is also responsible for marking an opponent in the vicinity of the ball. To fulfill both obligations the second defender must position himself or herself to cover the space behind the first defender and also to be able to challenge for the ball should it be passed to the opponent he or she is marking. The angle and distance of defensive cover in relation to the first defender is of critical importance.

The Angle of Cover

The second defender should not be directly behind the first defender, because from that position he or she will not have a clear view of the ball and will not be able to quickly readjust to the attacker's movements. The second defender should get into a position to form an angle between the ball and the opponent he or she is marking (Figure 10.2). In that manner he or she can protect the space behind the first defender as well as mark an opposing player.

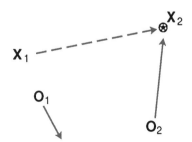

Figure 10.2 Proper angle of cover for the second defender.

The Distance of Cover

The second defender must be in a position to step up and challenge an opponent who has beaten the first defender on the dribble. To determine the correct distance of cover the second defender must take into account the position of the ball and the position of the opponent that the second defender is marking.

In general, the farther the ball is from the defender's goal, the greater the distance of cover can be. The space between the first and second defenders should be reduced as the ball moves closer to the defenders' goal. For example, if the ball is within 20 yards of your goal the proper distance of cover might be only 2 or 3 yards, whereas 6 to 8 yards might be appropriate if the ball is in the midfield area.

Remember that the second defender is responsible for marking an opponent as well as protecting the space behind the first defender. The closer that opponent is to the ball the tighter the distance of cover should be (Figure 10.3). The distance of cover should be increased as the player to be marked moves farther from the ball (Figure 10.4).

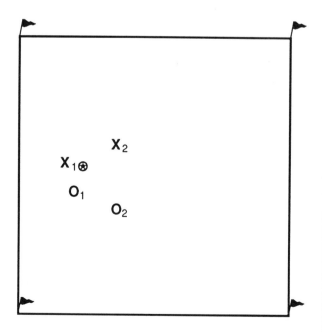

Figure 10.3 Distance of cover when the opponent is close to the ball.

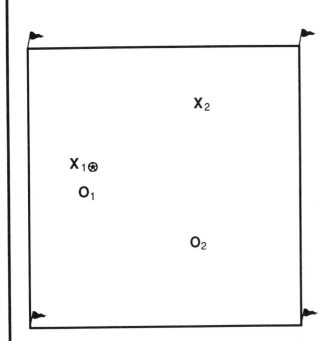

Figure 10.4 Distance of cover when the opponent is farther from the ball.

HOW TO EXECUTE BALANCE IN DEFENSE

While the first defender challenges for the ball and the second defender provides cover, the third defender is responsible for providing balance in defense. He or she should be positioned along an imaginary diagonal line that begins at the ball and extends toward the goalpost farthest from the ball. The third defender can accomplish three important objectives from that position along the line of balance: (a) protect the space behind the defense, (b) keep the ball in view at all times, and (c) keep the opponent he or she is marking in view (see Figure 10.5). Figure 10.6 presents small group defense strategies.

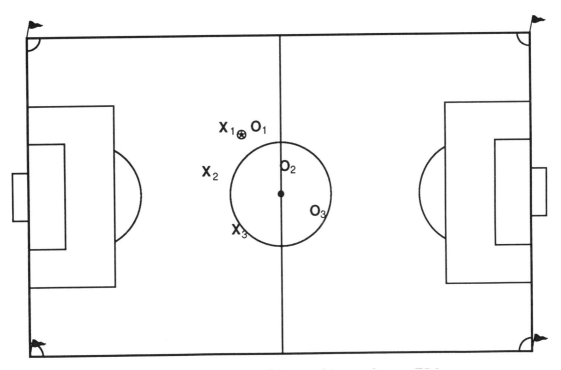

Figure 10.5 Positions of the first, second, and third defenders along the line of balance.

Figure 10.6 Keys to Success:
Small Group
Strategies
in Defense

Preparation Phase

First Defender

1. Position yourself goal-side and face player with ball ____
2. Assume proper defensive posture ____
3. Maintain balance and control ____
4. Vision focused on ball ____

Second Defender

1. Occupy space behind first defender ____
2. Position yourself at proper angle ____
3. Position yourself at proper distance ____
4. Mark opponent in vicinity of ball ____
5. Keep ball and opponent in view ____

Third Defender

1. Move into space diagonally behind second defender ____
2. Position yourself along line of balance ____
3. Keep ball and nearby opponents in view ____

Execution Phase

First Defender

1. Delay dribbler's forward progress ____
2. Force dribbler toward sideline ____
3. Force dribbler into covering defender ____
4. Challenge for ball ____
5. Gain possession of ball ____

Second Defender

1. Confront dribbler if first defender beaten ____
2. Prevent passes through space behind first defender ____

Third Defender

1. Prevent long diagonal passes ____
2. Maintain proper distance from second defender ____

Follow-Through Phase

First Defender	Second Defender	Third Defender
1. Move forward with ball ____ 2. Pass ball to open teammate ____ 3. Move into attacking support position ____	1. Assume role of first defender if original first defender beaten ____ 2. Initiate counterattack after gaining possession of ball ____	1. Adjust position with relation to movement of ball ____

Detecting Errors in Small Group Defensive Strategies

Defensive cover and balance require coordinated movement by the first, second, and third defenders. Poor communication between these players can lead to problems if one does not correctly read the play of the others. Most errors are due to incorrect timing of the tackle by the first defender or incorrect positioning by the second or third defender.

ERROR ⊘   **CORRECTION**

The First Defender

1. The first defender unsuccessfully attempts to tackle the ball before the second defender is properly positioned.

2. The first defender allows the dribbler to push the ball past him or her into space not covered by the second defender.

1. The first defender should not attempt to challenge for possession of the ball until he or she is supported by a second defender.

2. The first defender should adjust his or her position so as to force the dribbler into the space covered by the second defender. If that is not possible he or she should attempt to force the dribbler into the space near the sideline.

ERROR   **CORRECTION**

The Second Defender

1. The second defender positions himself or herself directly behind the first defender.

2. The second defender is positioned too far from the first defender so that he or she cannot close quickly enough to challenge the dribbler should the first defender be beaten.

The Third Defender

1. The third defender does not provide adequate balance away from the ball.

2. The third defender is positioned too close to the second defender and as a result is vulnerable to the long cross-field pass into the space behind him or her.

1. The second defender cannot prevent a pass through the space beside the first defender if he or she is positioned directly behind the first defender. The second defender should be positioned diagonally from the ball in the space behind and to the side of the first defender.

2. The second defender must consider the ability of the first defender as well as the ability of the opponent when determining the proper covering distance.

1. The third defender should be positioned diagonally behind and to the side of the second defender. From that position he or she will be able to keep the ball and nearby opponents in sight and at the same time prevent a penetrating pass into the space behind the second defender.

2. The third defender should not be concerned about providing close cover for the second defender. If the ball is played into the space behind the second defender, the third defender will have sufficient time to close the space while the ball is in flight.

Defensive Cover and Balance Drills

1. Cover the Goal

Select two classmates to participate with you in this exercise. Play in a 10-by-15-yard grid. Position a goal 4 yards wide on one endline of the grid. Position a classmate in each corner of the grid opposite the goal. You are in the center of the grid with the goal behind you. Your classmates must stay in their corners of the grid throughout the drill; they cannot move forward. They attempt to quickly pass the ball back and forth until an open lane is created through which they can pass the ball into the goal. Your objective is to prevent the ball from being passed through to the goal by quickly readjusting your cover position in relation to the movement of the ball. Your opponents are awarded 1 point for each ball they pass through the goal. You are awarded 1 point each time you prevent a pass from going through the goal. Play for 5 minutes.

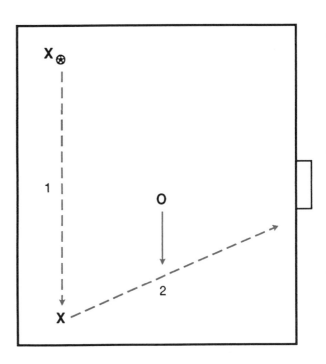

Success Goal = score more points than opponents

Your Score =

(#) _____ your points

(#) _____ opponent's points

2. Two Versus Two Drill

Select three classmates to participate with you in this exercise. Organize into teams of two players each. Mark off a 15-by-20-yard grid and position a goal 4 yards wide at each end of the grid. Play two versus two within the grid. Your team begins with possession of the ball. The primary emphasis of this exercise is on defensive cover. The first defender of the defending team should pressure the opponent with the ball; the second defender should position himself or herself to prevent the ball from being kicked past the first defender through the goal. The second defender must also be in correct position to challenge for the ball should it be passed to the opponent he or she is marking. A team scores a goal by passing the ball through the opposing team's goal. Play until one team has scored 10 goals.

Success Goal = allow fewer goals than opponent

Your Score =

(#) ____ goals allowed by your team

(#) ____ goals allowed by opponent

3. *Three Versus Two Drill*

Select four classmates to participate with you in this exercise. Organize two teams—you and a classmate join to form one team and the three remaining players form the opposing team. Play within a 15-by-15-yard grid area. Your opponents attempt to keep the ball away from your team by combination passing within the grid. The opposing team is awarded 1 point each time it completes 10 passes in succession, and 2 points if it completes a pass to a team-mate that splits (goes between) you and your teammate. Your team is awarded 1 point each time you win possession of the ball. Remember that the first defender should challenge the opponent with the ball while the second defender plays cover to prevent the through pass. When you or your teammate win possession of the ball, give it back to the opposing team and continue playing. Play for 10 minutes and keep track of the points scored.

Success Goal = score more points than opponents

Your Score =

(#) ____ your team's points

(#) ____ opponent's points

4. *Three Versus Two Plus One*

Select five classmates to participate with you in this exercise. Organize two teams of three players each. Play on a 20-by-30-yard field with a goal 4 yards wide positioned at each end of the playing area. Flip a coin to determine which team begins with possession of the ball. The team with the ball attacks with three players while the opposing team defends with two players and a goalkeeper. Because the defenders are outnumbered (3 vs. 2), the first defender must challenge for the ball while the second defender plays in a cover position to mark space behind the first defender. Defenders must constantly readjust their positions with relation to the movement of the ball. Teams switch roles if the defending team gains possession of the ball and after a goal is scored. The former defending team attacks with three players while the former attacking team drops one player into goal and defends with two players. Once the drill begins play should be continuous as teams attack with three players and defend with two field players and a goalkeeper. Goals are scored by kicking the ball through the oppo-nent's goal. Play for 15 minutes.

Success Goal = allow fewer goals than opponents

Your Score =

(#) _____ goals allowed by your team

(#) _____ goals allowed by opponent

5. Changing the Line of Balance

This drill gives defenders practice in changing their line of balance in relation to the changing position of the ball. Play on one half of a regulation field or in a large gymnasium. Use cones or flags to mark a regulation-width goal on one endline. Select five classmates to participate with you in this exercise. Position three players (targets) in a straight line across the field approximately 35 yards from the goal. These players should face the goal and stand approximately 15 yards apart. One of the targets has possession of the ball. You and the remaining two players position yourselves to defend the goal. The objective of the drill is for the three target players to pass the ball to each other, constantly changing the location of the ball (point of attack). You and your teammates (first, second, and third defenders) must adjust your positions in response to the changing position of the ball to prevent the target players from passing the ball through your defense into the goal. The target players are not permitted to move forward with the ball, but they are allowed to pass the ball forward into the goal if they see an open lane in your defense. Target players are awarded 1 point each time they pass the ball through the defense into the goal. All passes must be along the ground. Play for 5 minutes and keep track of points allowed.

Success Goal = 5 or fewer points allowed in 5 minutes

Your Score = (#) _____ points allowed

6. Prevent the Killer Pass

Select five classmates to participate with you in this exercise. Organize two teams of three players each. Use cones or flags to mark off a field area of 20 by 30 yards. Flip a coin to determine which team has possession of the ball to begin the game. The team with the ball attempts to maintain possession from the opposing team within the confines of the field area. Points are scored in two ways. A team is awarded 1 point if its players can combine for eight passes in succession. A team is awarded 2 points if its players can complete a ''killer'' pass, one that splits (goes between) two defending players. Defending players must work in unison to provide cover and balance to prevent the killer pass. Once the game begins play is continuous; when a team loses possession of the ball its players must immediately defend. Play for 15 minutes.

Success Goal = allow fewer points than opponent

Your Score =

(#) _____ points allowed by your team

(#) _____ points allowed by opponent

7. *Defending in an Outnumbered Situation*

Select seven classmates to participate with you in this exercise. Organize one team of five players; you and the remaining two players join to form the outnumbered team. Use cones or flags to mark off a field area of 30 by 40 yards. Position a goal 6 yards wide at the center of one endline. Position two small goals, each 3 yards wide, at opposite ends of the other endline. Do not use goalkeepers in this drill. The team with five players defends the large goal and attempts to score in either of the small goals. Your team defends the two small goals and attempts to score in the large goal. Your team must use cover and balance to offset the attacking maneuvers of the opposing team. The team with five players is awarded 1 point for each goal scored. Your team, because it is outnumbered, is awarded 2 points for each goal scored. Play for 10 minutes, then reorganize the teams so that different players make up the outnumbered team.

Success Goals =

do not allow any goals as a result of a pass that splits the defense

score more points than opponent

Your Score =

(#) _____ goals scored by opponents as a result of a pass that splits the defense

(#) _____ points scored by your team

(#) _____ points scored by opponents

Small Group Defensive Strategies Keys to Success Checklist

Ask your teacher, your coach, or a classmate to observe you in defensive situations. Alternate playing first, second, and third defender.

The observer can use the checklist in Figure 10.6 to evaluate your performance and provide corrective feedback.

Step 11   Attacking as a Team

Team tactics ultimately deal with the concepts of space and time. You have learned the important relationship between those two factors: the time available for individual skill execution and decision making is directly proportional to the space available to the player with the ball. In other words, the more space available, the more time you have to receive, control, pass, or shoot the ball. Attacking team tactics are designed to create space and time on the soccer field. Because defending players position themselves to restrict space and eliminate passing options, the attacking team must use various movement patterns to create more open space, to provide as many passing options as possible, and ultimately to finish each attack with a score. This can be accomplished only if all players have a clear understanding of the basic principles that underlie attacking soccer.

WHY IS ATTACKING AS A TEAM IMPORTANT?

The precise teamwork required to create scoring opportunities can occur only if individual players collectively focus and combine their efforts toward a common objective. Each player must be prepared to fulfill specific responsibilities in his or her team's attacking scheme. These reponsibilities include such things as running without the ball to create space for a teammate, supporting the teammate with the ball, making a penetrating run through the opposing defense, and possibly even finishing the attack with a score. Your ability to choose the correct course of action from a multitude of options will play a vital role in your overall contribution to the team's attacking efforts. Improve your decision making and you will improve individual as well as team performance.

HOW TO ATTACK AS A TEAM

To improve your decision making you must establish guidelines on which to base your decisions. The following principles conceptualize the goals and objectives of attacking soccer and provide a logical process for achieving them.

Player Movement With and Without the Ball

Time motion studies demonstrate that the typical soccer player has possession of the ball for only 3 to 4 minutes during a 90-minute match. For more than 86 minutes you will be without the ball! It is obvious that you must do something more than just occupy space during that time.

You should be moving constantly when your team has the ball. Your movement should be purposeful and carried out with a specific objective in mind, such as creating space in which to receive a pass, drawing defending players into poor positions, supporting the player with the ball, or clearing space for a fellow teammate. Your objective may be merely to confuse the marking defender. Whatever the purpose, you can use a variety of different running patterns to achieve your aim. The following section describes some common types of runs.

Diagonal runs penetrate diagonally through the defense. You can begin your run in the flank area and travel through the center of the defense, or you can begin from a central area of the field and move toward the flanks. In either case, diagonal runs have several advantages over runs that travel flat across the field. Diagonal runs penetrate through the defense and force defending players to mark you, possibly drawing opponents into poor defending positions. A diagonal run may also clear an area of opponents so a teammate can move forward into the space created. Finally, a diagonal run from the flank through the center of the defense puts you in an excellent position to penetrate and score should you receive a pass while moving through the defense (Figure 11.1).

Checking runs create space between you and the defender marking you. Bluff a run forward past the player marking you, then suddenly

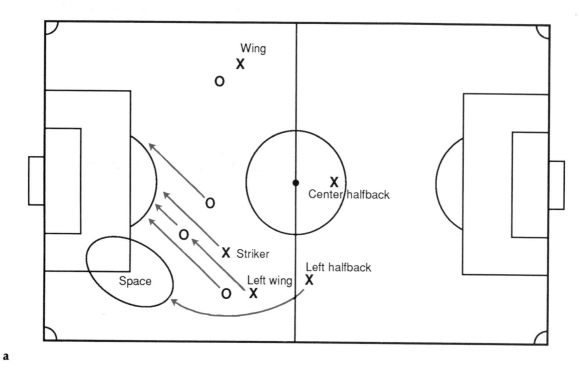

a

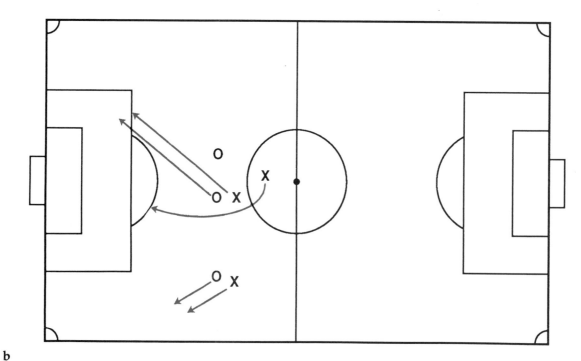

b

Figure 11.1 Examples of diagonal runs.

check back toward the ball. Because the defender has been taught to maintain a position goalside of you, space is created between you and the defender when you suddenly stop and check back toward the ball. You can take advantage of the available space to receive the ball and turn to face the defender (Figure 11.2).

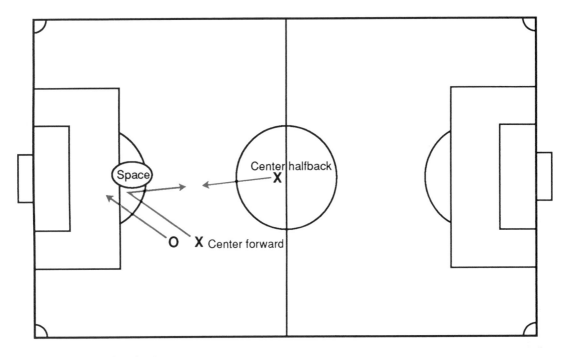

Figure 11.2 Example of a checking run.

Combination Play for Width and Depth

The attacking team can force the defending team to cover a larger field area by combining effective passing of the ball with proper positioning of players. Passes should vary in type, distance, speed, and direction to unbalance the opposing team. Attacking players should also position themselves to provide width and depth in their team's system of play.

You have already learned that the player with the ball should have three teammates in close support positions. A teammate should be positioned on each side and slightly ahead of the player with the ball with another support player positioned a few yards behind the ball. The function of the player behind the ball is to provide depth in the attack and to do what the player with the ball is not always able to do—pass the ball forward. For example, if the player with the ball is challenged by an opponent and is not in a position to pass the ball forward, he or she can pass the ball back to the trailing support player, who can then pass it forward to another teammate.

Your team can create space within the opposing team's defense by stretching itself vertically up and down the field. This is also an example of depth in attack and is accomplished by positioning a minimum of one or two players well ahead of the ball (Figure 11.3). These front-running individuals generally spearhead the attack, playing as targets who receive and control the ball until teammates can sprint forward in support.

Width in attack is generally provided by players away from the ball, commonly known as *weak-side players*. Weak-side players position themselves on the side of the field opposite the ball to stretch the opposing defense from one sideline to the other. Width in attack

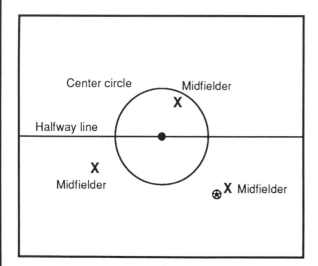

Figure 11.3 Width and depth in attack.

forces defenders to cover a larger field area and creates space within the defense. Weak-side players can also make penetrating runs from their flank positions through the center of the opposing defense.

Improvisation

Improvisation in attack is best exemplified by the tactical use of dribbling skills. All players should realize the important role dribbling can play in their team's attacking scheme. The player who can successfully execute dribbling skills at opportune times in specific areas of the field can be the most dangerous weapon in a team's attacking arsenal. On the other hand, excessive dribbling at inappropriate times or in the wrong area of the field can destroy a team's attacking efforts.

To understand the tactical use of dribbling skills as they apply to different areas of the field, we can divide the playing field into three sections—the defending third, the midfield third, and the attacking third (Figure 11.4).

Defending Third—Area of No Risk

Always weigh risk against safety when deciding whether or not to dribble. The defending third of the field nearest your goal is an area where you should take little or no risk. Do not attempt to beat an opponent on the dribble in the defending third. Loss of possession in this area may cost your team a goal. Think "safety first" in the defending third.

Midfield Third—Area of Moderate Risk

Players can use dribbling skills with greater frequency and more positive results in the

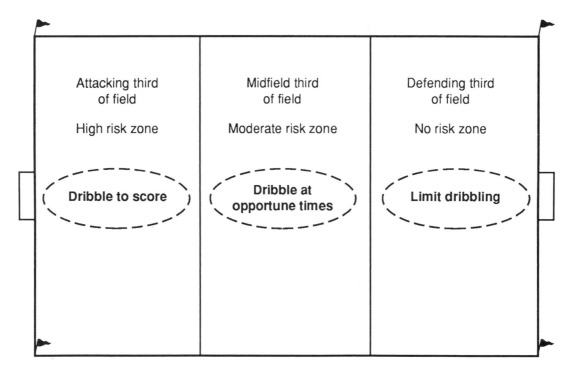

Figure 11.4 Risk versus safety in the three sections of the field.

midfield third of the field. If you can beat an opponent on the dribble in this area, you will create a numerical superiority in attacking players as your team moves toward the opponent's goal. In the event that you lose the ball to an opponent, he or she is not within immediate scoring range of your goal. Even so, excessive dribbling in the midfield third is not warranted because it tends to slow the attack and makes play predictable.

Attacking Third—Area of Greatest Risk

The use of dribbling skills can be most effective in the attacking third of the field nearest the opponent's goal. The benefits of the risk outweigh those of safety in that area because if you can beat an opponent on the dribble, you will create an excellent scoring opportunity for your team. In addition, loss of possession will not pose an immediate threat to your own goal. Learn to recognize the situations that warrant dribbling and take advantage of them. The result may be the ultimate aim of every attack—a goal scored.

Total Team Support

As you have learned, support refers to the movement of players toward the area of the ball. The player with the ball should always have a minimum of two teammates nearby as passing options. The concept of support can be extended to the entire team if we consider each player as supporting a teammate and in return being supported by one or more teammates.

Soccer is sometimes called a game of triangles. This analogy refers to the support positioning of players as they move throughout the field space. If all 10 field players position themselves at the correct depth and angle of support with respect to nearby teammates, then the organization of players does resemble a series of interconnected triangles. These player triangles are not static, however. Players must constantly readjust their positions based on the location of the ball.

Total team support can be achieved only if all players move up and down the field as a unit. There should be no more than 40 to 45 yards between the last defender in the back line and the deepest penetrating attacker in the front line (Figure 11.5a and b).

Finish the Attack

Ideally every attack should culminate in a goal scored. Realistically we know that just isn't possible. Ten opposing field players and a goalkeeper are doing everything within their power to prevent your team from scoring. As a consequence, the individual who can consistently put the ball in the back of the opponent's net is an extremely valuable player for his or her team. Success requires a combination of skill, determination, courage, and intelligent tactical play.

I've heard many coaches say that goal scorers are born, not made. They point out the intangible qualities that the great goal scorers seem to possess, qualities like anticipation, precise timing, composure, and the ability to be in the right place at the right time. It is no secret that certain individuals have more innate ability than others. But all players, regardless of their inherent strengths and weaknesses, can improve their goal-scoring abilities through dedicated practice. Develop the ability to shoot with power and accuracy under the pressures of game competition. Learn to release your shot quickly with either foot and from all different positions.

Improving your individual level of skill is not the only factor of concern. Collectively you and your teammates must work together to create opportunities in the most dangerous scoring zones—the central areas of the field that provide a wide shooting angle to the goal. Shots taken front and center of the goal are most likely to score. Shots taken from the flank areas, where the shooting angle is reduced, rarely beat the goalkeeper (Figure 11.6).

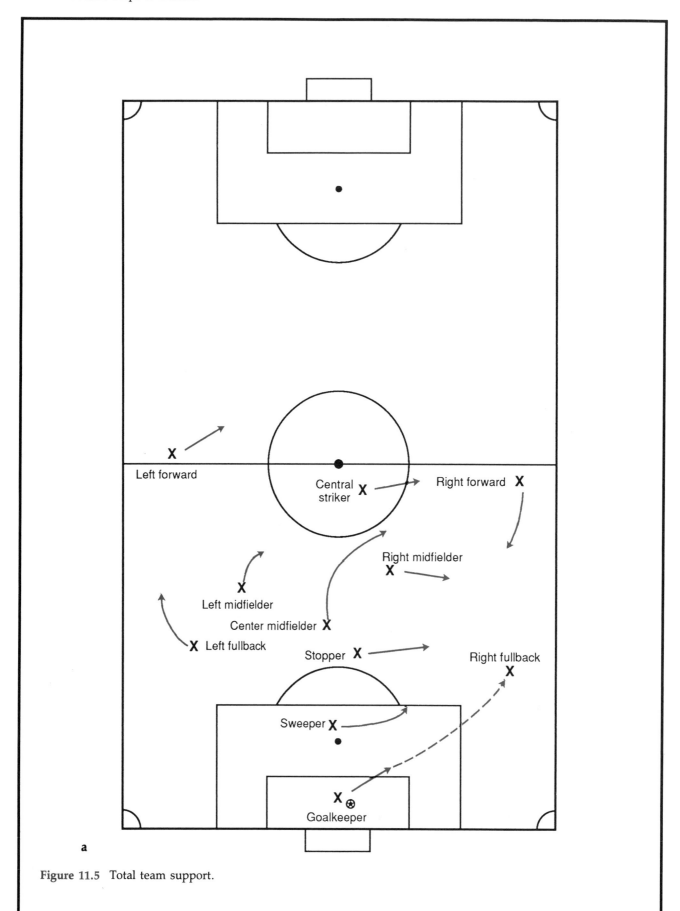

Figure 11.5   Total team support.

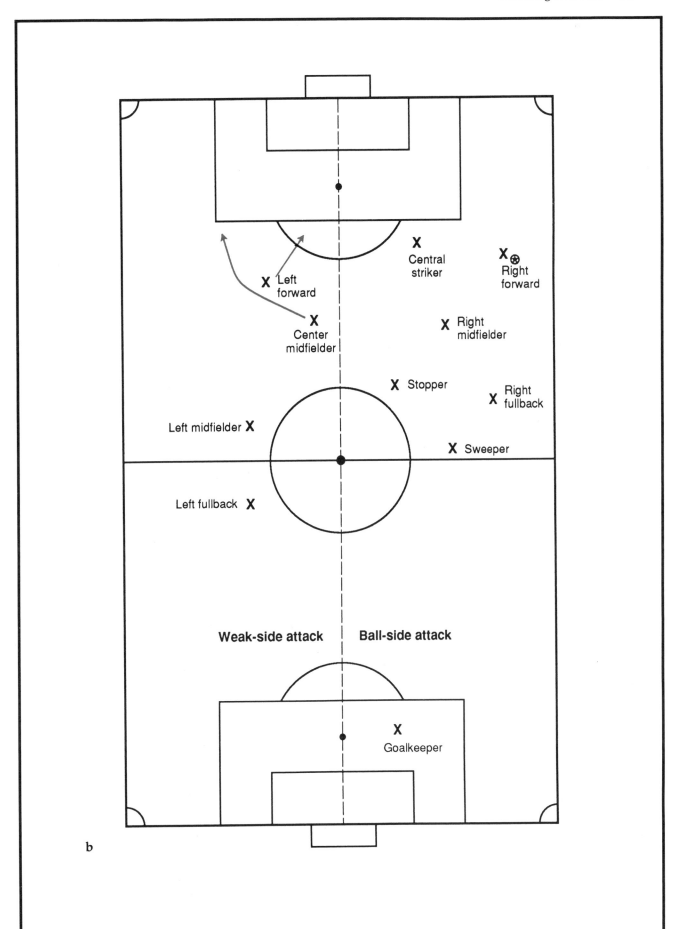

X Central striker

X Right forward

X Left forward

X Right midfielder

X Center midfielder

X Stopper

X Right fullback

Left midfielder **X**

X Sweeper

Left fullback **X**

Weak-side attack   **Ball-side attack**

X Goalkeeper

b

Figure 11.6 Scoring zones.

Attacking Principles of Play Drill

Six Versus Four Drill

Select 10 classmates to participate with you in this exercise. Designate four players as defenders, one as a goalkeeper, and the remaining five players and you as attackers. Select 1 additional classmate or your teacher to be the scorekeeper. Use cones or flags to mark off an area of 50 by 60 yards. Position a regulation goal on one endline and position two minigoals 20 yards apart on the other endline. If a regulation field is available, play on one half of the field. Position a goalkeeper in the regulation goal; do not use goalkeepers in the minigoals. Your team gets possession of the ball to begin the game.

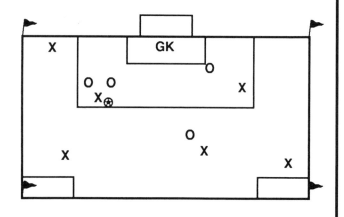

Your team tries to score in the regulation goal. Points can be scored in a variety of ways reflecting the proper execution of one or more principles of attack. Points are awarded for the following:

- 1 point for eight passes in succession without loss of possession
- 1 point for a successful give and go (combination) pass

- 1 point for a shot on goal saved by the goalkeeper
- 1 additional point if the shot was taken from a central location—within the width of the penalty area
- 2 points for each goal scored from within 18 yards of the goal
- 2 points for each goal scored off a ball crossed from the flank
- 3 points for each goal scored when an individual player beats a defender on the dribble, shoots, and scores
- 3 points for each goal scored from a distance of 20 yards or more from the goal

The defending team is awarded 1 point each time a defending player wins possession of the ball, and 3 points each time it counterattacks and kicks the ball through one of the minigoals. Play is continuous for 20 minutes. Use the Offensive Team and Defensive Team scorecards for recording points during play.

Offensive Team Scorecard

8 passes in succession	___ × 1 point	= ___ points
Successful give and go passes	___ × 1 point	= ___ points
Shots saved by goalkeeper	___ × 1 point	= ___ points
Shots taken from central location	___ × 1 point	= ___ points
Goals scored within 18 yards	___ × 2 points	= ___ points
Goals scored off crosses from flank	___ × 2 points	= ___ points
Goals scored by beating defender on dribble	___ × 3 points	= ___ points
Goals scored from 20+ yards	___ × 3 points	= ___ points
	Total	= ___ points

Defensive Team Scorecard

Wins possession of ball	___ × 1 point	= ___ points
Goals through minigoals	___ × 3 points	= ___ points
	Total	= ___ points

Step 12 Defending as a Team

You have already mastered the defending tactics and strategies used in individual and small group situations. The next step is to incorporate all of these into an overall plan for team defense.

WHY IS DEFENDING AS A TEAM IMPORTANT?

Just as offensive success in soccer depends on teamwork, so does defensive success. One or two outstanding defensive players cannot stop a team with a balanced offense. Teammates must work together in an organized manner to play defense effectively. Each player must fulfill specific duties if an attack is to be stopped.

HOW TO DEFEND AS A TEAM

The organization of a strong team defense depends on several factors. Players must be physically fit so they can maintain a consistent level of performance for an entire game. Players must be able to successfully tackle and win possession of the ball. Team defense also depends to a large extent on the decisions that players make in response to the ever-changing situations that occur during play. Decisions such as when to challenge for the ball, where to position for optimum cover and balance, and when to move forward into the attack all affect the overall success of the team's defensive efforts.

Poor individual decisions ultimately lead to poor team defense and goals scored against your team. You can improve your decision making by clearly understanding what your teammates are collectively trying to accomplish when the opposing team has possession of the ball. Base your decisions on an understanding of your role within the overall team structure. The following principles of team defense provide guidelines for your decision making. It is essential that all players base their decisions and actions on the same criteria.

These principles of team defense apply to all systems of play and progress through a logical sequence from the moment a team loses possession of the ball until the instant it regains possession and goes on the attack.

Immediate Pressure in the Area of the Ball

The few seconds immediately following loss of possession are critical for the defending team. Players may be disorganized because they are in transition between attacking and defending modes of play. The team is most vulnerable to a swift counterattack during that transition period. To prevent a counterattack and possible score the defending player(s) nearest to the ball should initiate an immediate challenge to regain possession. If they can delay the opponent even for only a few moments, then their teammates will have extra time in which to regroup and organize the defense.

Fall Back and Delay

While players in the area of the ball are applying pressure, the remaining defending players should swiftly retreat to a position between the ball and their goal. From a goal-side position they will be able to keep the ball and the opponents they are marking in view (Figure 12.1).

Limit Space by Compacting the Defense

The defending team's highest priority should be eliminating the open space front and center of its goal. This is the area from which most goals are scored. Players should also try to eliminate open lanes within the defense through which attacking players can penetrate with the ball. Consolidating players in the most dangerous scoring zones has become an accepted tactic to achieve both these objectives. Defending players should funnel inward

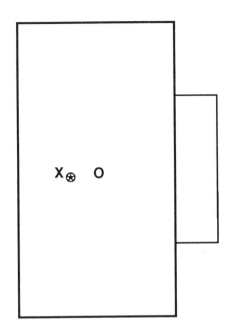

Figure 12.1 Defender in a goalside position.

toward the central areas of the field as they retreat to their positions goalside of the ball. From a central position they will be able to effectively control the most dangerous scoring areas and if necessary can still move into the flank areas to challenge an opponent with the ball (Figure 12.2).

Depth in Defense

Each defending player should be supported from behind by one or more teammates, a concept commonly known as *cover* or *depth*. As defenders withdraw and consolidate in the most dangerous scoring zones they must position themselves to provide cover for each other. Proper positioning limits the space between defenders and also ensures that defenders are not aligned flat across the field. A lack of depth makes the defending team vulnerable to passes slotted diagonally through the defense (Figure 12.3).

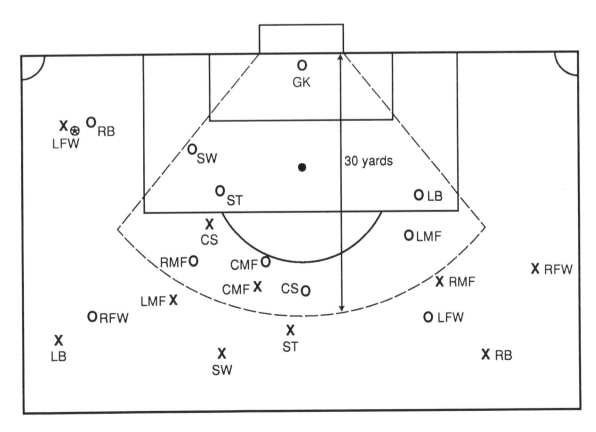

Figure 12.2 Compacting the defense.

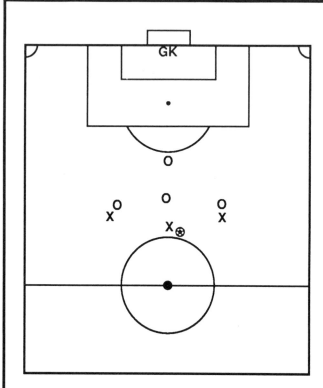

Figure 12.3 Depth in defense.

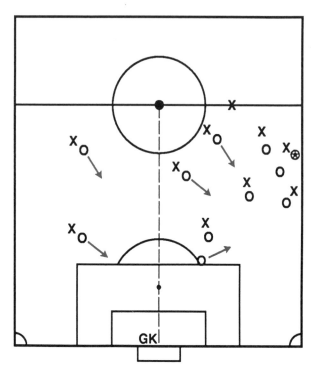

Figure 12.4 Balance in defense.

Deny Opponents Space Behind the Defense

As defending players position themselves to limit the available space within the defense, they must also protect the open space that exists behind the defense. As you have already learned, this is accomplished through the defensive principle of balance. Players on the side of the field opposite the ball should be positioned along an imaginary diagonal line beginning at the ball and traveling toward the far post of the goal. From that position they can protect the space behind the defense and at the same time keep the ball and opponents in sight (Figure 12.4).

Eliminate Passing Options

As defending players position themselves to limit space within and behind the defense, they should also try to limit the number of passing options available to the opponent with the ball. This objective can be accomplished in two ways. The first is tight marking of all opposing players in the area of the ball. The player with the ball will be forced to attempt a longer pass if nearby teammates are unavail-

able as passing options. The chance of error is greater with a long pass. A second method of eliminating passing options is positioning defenders in the passing lanes between attackers, thereby forcing the player with the ball to chip it over defenders or pass it wide to flank areas. In either instance the advantage shifts to the defense. Lofted passes are more difficult to successfully execute than ground passes and the risk of error is greater. Also, from a defensive perspective, the flank areas are the least critical space to protect because the shooting angle to the goal is very narrow.

Make Play Predictable

Attacking players will try to disguise their intentions to confuse defenders. You can counter this tactic by making the play of the attacking team as predictable as possible. The more predictable the play of opponents the easier it is for you and your defending teammates to anticipate and make appropriate decisions. This principle is actually an extension of the previous principle because by reducing the number of passing options available to an opponent, you actually make his or her play more predictable. Once you know what the opponent can't do, then you can better anticipate what that player will do in a given situation. Another method of making play predictable is forcing the opponent to move in one direction or another. If possible, force him or her toward the sideline of the field. There are two reasons for doing this: The space available to the opponent is limited by the sideline, and the area through which the opponent can pass the ball forward is reduced.

Challenge for the Ball

At this point the defending team should be in excellent position to challenge for possession of the ball. Defending players are positioned to provide cover and balance, the most dangerous scoring zones are protected, and the play of the attacking team has been made as predictable as possible. The player nearest the ball can now attempt to tackle the ball at the appropriate moment.

Team Defense Drill

Six Versus Four Drill

Organize your classmates as you did for the Six Versus Four Drill in the previous step. This time, you play on the defensive team. Award the attacking team possession of the ball to begin the game.

The attacking team tries to score in the regulation goal while your team and the goalkeeper defend. The attacking team scores 2 points by kicking the ball past the goalkeeper through the goal, or scores 1 point by taking a shot on the goal that the goalkeeper saves.

Your (defending) team scores points by successfully executing several of the basic principles of defense. The defending team is awarded 1 point for each of the following: (a) a successful tackle of the ball, (b) intercepting a pass, and (c) counterattacking and kicking the ball through one of the minigoals. Play for 20 minutes and keep score.

Defensive Team Scorecard

Successful tackles ____ × 1 point = ____ points

Passes intercepted ____ × 1 point = ____ points

Goals in minigoals ____ × 1 point = ____ points

Total = ____ points

Offensive Team Scorecard

Shots saved by goalkeeper ____ × 1 point = ____ points

Goals scored ____ × 2 points = ____ points

Total = ____ points

Step 13 **Team Organization and Communication**

Now that you have mastered the basic offensive and defensive skills and understand the tactics and strategies used for team play, you are ready to put all your knowledge and ability to use in a regulation game. Before you do, however, you should develop a general understanding of systems of play. A *system of play* refers to the tactical organization and responsibilities of the 10 field players. The basic skills and principles of play that you have learned to this point are universal to all systems, although individual responsibilities may differ from system to system.

WHY IS TEAM ORGANIZATION IMPORTANT?

A system defines each players's role within the overall structure of the team. For example, two players may both be listed as midfielders but actually fill substantially different roles on their team. One might be a defensive midfielder assigned the task of marking the opposing team's playmaker, whereas the other might be primarily an attacking midfielder expected to create scoring opportunities for his or her teammates. To achieve the cohesion and teamwork necessary for successful team performance, each player must understand his or her role within the team.

HOW SYSTEMS ARE ORGANIZED

Players are usually designated as defenders, midfielders, or forwards. As a general rule, all systems have at least three defenders, two midfielders, and two forwards. Because a full team is made up of 10 field players and a goalkeeper, that leaves 3 field players to be positioned as the coach sees fit. Variations in how these 3 players are used results in different formations and player responsibilities.

A number of systems have come and gone throughout soccer's long history. Which system is best? It depends on the natures and abilities of the players who make up the team. A system that works for one team might not be appropriate for another. The system should be chosen to highlight team strengths and minimize player weaknesses. The following discussion focuses on four of the more popular systems of the modern era—the 4-2-4, the 4-4-2, the 4-3-3, and the 3-5-2. In a description of a system of play, the first number refers to the defending players, the second number to the midfield players, and the third to the forwards or attackers. The goalkeeper is not included in the numbering of players.

The 4-2-4 System

The 4-2-4 alignment was first introduced during the 1958 World Cup games by the Brazilian National Team. Blessed with a number of great players, including the incomparable Pele, Brazil's team captured the hearts and support of soccer fans around the world as it won the World Cup championship. The 4-2-4 system quickly gained widespread popularity as coaches tried to emulate the success of the Brazilians. It was the first system to emphasize player mobility and interchanging of positions. All players had a role in both defense and attack. The 4-2-4 introduced the philosophy of "total soccer" because players were not limited to playing one specific position on the field.

The four defenders are organized with a sweeper, one central (stopper) back, and right and left wing defenders. The wing defenders and stopper back are generally assigned one-on-one marking responsibilities whereas the sweeper's role is to provide cover for the other three defenders. The sweeper is designated as the "free" back and is not assigned a specific opponent to mark.

Two midfield players, or linkmen, function as the connecting thread between the defenders and forwards. The midfielders must support their forwards when on the attack and must also provide a line of defense in front of the defenders when the opposing team has the ball.

The forwards are usually organized with two flank players, or wingers, and two central forwards, or strikers. One of the strikers is usually positioned deep in the opponent's defense, near the opposing sweeper, to spearhead the attack. The other forward is usually withdrawn to provide help in the midfield when needed (see Figure 13.1).

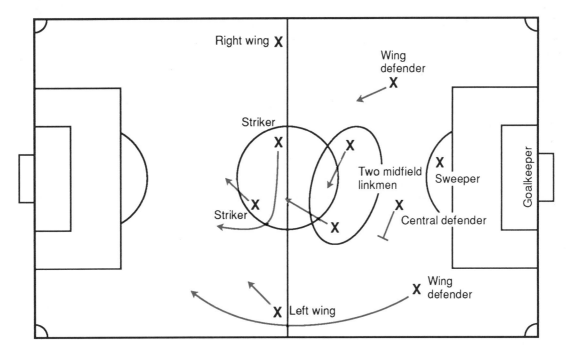

Figure 13.1 4-2-4 system.

The 4-4-2 System

Control of the midfield area is vital to team success. An obvious concern with the 4-2-4 system is the tremendous work load placed on the two midfielders. In an attempt to provide greater midfield control, innovative coaches began to withdraw their wing forwards into the midfield to create a 4-4-2 alignment. Theoretically, with four players controlling the midfield a team can dominate play in that area from both attacking and defending perspectives.

Player responsibilities in the 4-4-2 system are somewhat similar to those in the 4-2-4. The four backs are aligned in similar fashion with a sweeper providing cover behind three marking defenders. The midfielders are usually positioned with one on each flank and two in the center of the field. The playing styles and abilities of the two central midfielders should complement each other. One is usually desig-

nated as the attacking midfielder whereas the other is assigned a more defensive role. There are no true wingers in the 4-4-2. The wing midfielders are expected to move forward and provide width in the attack when their team has possession of the ball. If the wing midfielders do not make the immediate transition from defense to attack, then the 4-4-2 takes on a defensive orientation (see Figure 13.2).

The 4-3-3 System

The 4-3-3 alignment evolved from efforts to create a balance between attack and defense while placing even greater emphasis on player mobility and interchanging of positions. The four defenders are organized in the same manner as in the 4-4-2 system with a sweeper playing behind the two wing defenders and the stopper back. The stopper back is usually assigned the task of marking the opposing team's central striker whereas the wing

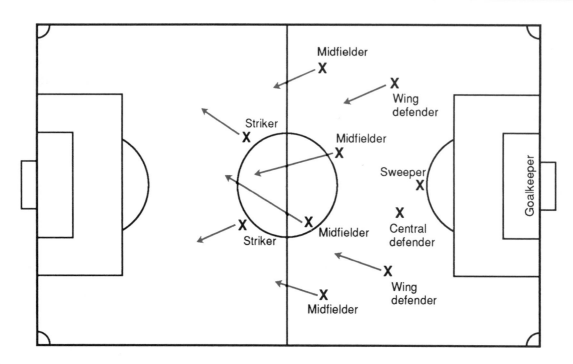

Figure 13.2 4-4-2 system.

defenders are matched against opponents in the flank areas.

The 4-3-3 uses one central midfielder who is flanked on each side by a wing midfielder. The center midfielder is a key player in this system. He or she must be a creative play-maker, possess good passing and dribbling skills, and also have the ability to move forward and score goals. On defense the center midfielder must be a strong tackler of the ball as well as a dominant player in the air.

Three forwards are stationed in the front-running positions. Two flank players, or wingers, provide width in attack and the central striker plays as a target in the middle. All three forwards must exhibit a great deal of mobility and must interchange their positions to confuse defenders and create space in which midfielders and defenders can move forward. The forwards are also responsible for scoring most, though not all, of the goals for their team.

The 4-3-3 system requires that defenders as well as midfielders be able to move forward and contribute to their team's attack. This is usually accomplished through the tactic of *overlapping runs*. Defending players move forward out of the back, overlap the team-

mate in front of them, and sprint ahead into a more dangerous attacking position. If the run is properly timed, overlapping defenders and midfielders can catch the opponents by surprise and create dangerous scoring opportunities (see Figure 13.3).

The 3-5-2 System

A recent development in the organization of players deploys three defenders, five midfielders, and two forwards. The defenders consist of a sweeper who plays behind two central defenders assigned the task of marking the opposing strikers. One of the midfielders assumes the role of the "windscreen," or anchor player, in front of the defense. Unlike the traditional defensive midfielder who usually marks a specific opponent, the anchor player uses zonal marking in the area in front of the central defenders. The anchor player's primary responsibility is to intercept passes and prevent opponents from penetrating through the center of the defense. The remaining four midfielders are usually deployed across the field, two centrally and two on the flanks, in front of the anchor player. The two forwards are usually positioned deep in the opposing defense as targets and are also re-

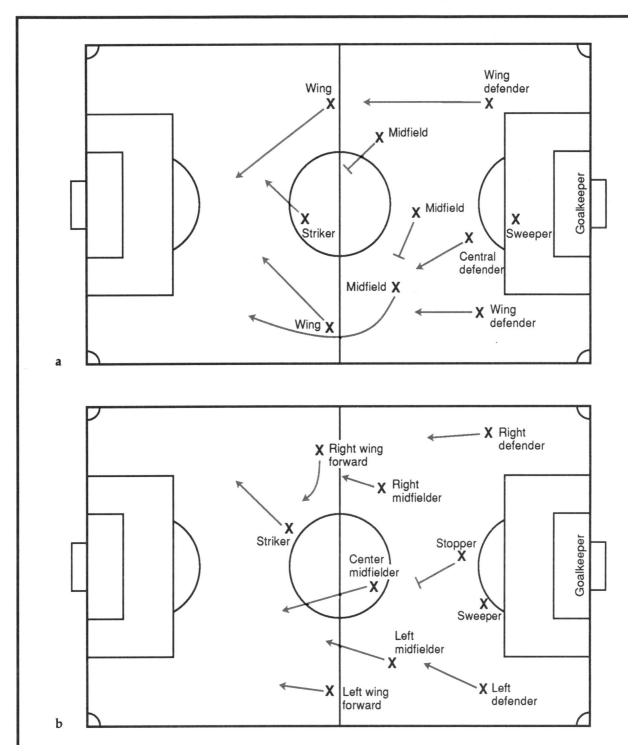

Figure 13.3   4-3-3 system.

quired to create open space for the midfielders through off-the-ball running patterns (see Figure 13.4).

SIGNALING FOR SUCCESS

The soccer field is not a quiet place. It is usually filled with constant chatter as players verbally communicate with each other during play. Communication is essential because you must work together with your teammates to achieve success. Your verbal commands can provide important information to teammates that will help in their decision making. For example, you can let a teammate know if an opponent is positioned behind him or

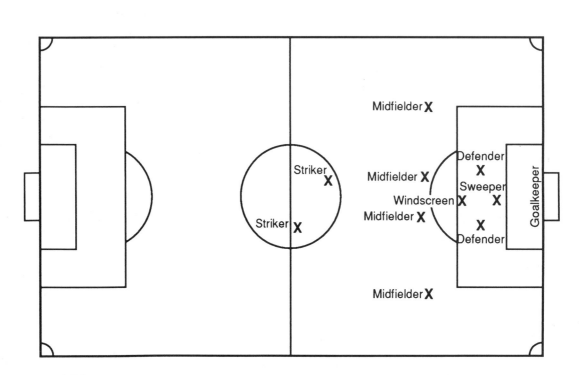

Figure 13.4 3-5-2 system.

her; whether to pass, dribble, or shoot the ball; or which opponent to mark. Your commands must be clear and decisive to avoid any confusion.

Follow these general guidelines when issuing verbal instructions:

1. Keep it simple—your comments should be concise and to the point.
2. Call early—provide your teammates sufficient time to respond.
3. Call loudly—your teammate doesn't have time to ask you to repeat what you said.

It is best to adopt a standard set of verbal signals to avoid misunderstandings. The following commands are common in soccer and should be understood by all players.

When on the attack:

- Call "man-on" when an opponent is directly behind a teammate who is receiving the ball. This will alert your teammate to shield the ball from the challenging defender.

- Call "turn" to indicate that a teammate has sufficient space to turn with the ball and face the opponent's goal.
- Call "one touch" to inform your teammate not to stop the ball but rather pass it on the first touch.
- Call "one-two" or "give and go" when you want your teammate to execute a give and go pass with you.
- Call "hold the ball" to indicate that your teammate should protect the ball from an opponent until supporting teammates arrive to help.
- Call "dummy it" when you want a teammate to let the ball roll past him or her to you.

When on defense:

- Call "mark-up" to inform a teammate to use one-on-one coverage of opponents.
- Call "close up" to instruct a teammate to reduce the space between himself or herself and the opponent with the ball.
- Call "weak side" to indicate that opponents are moving forward on the side of the field opposite the ball.

• Call "runner" to indicate that an opponent is running diagonally through the defense.

In addition to the preceding verbal signals, visual signals are also an effective means of communicating with teammates. Use your arms to point where you want the ball to be passed or where you want a teammate to move. You can even communicate with teammates in more subtle ways. A sudden glance in a specific direction or a slight nod of the head can inform teammates of your intentions. Visual signals are usually more difficult to interpret than verbal signals, however, and are generally used by players who have played together on the same team for a long time.

Team Organization Drill

The only real differences between the various systems of play are the roles assigned to individual players. The basic principles of attack and defense apply to all systems regardless of the alignment of players. In reality, if players adhere to the basic principles of play discussed earlier, all systems look virtually the same once the game begins. As a consequence there are no specific drills or exercises used to practice the individual systems.

However, there is a way that you and your teammates can become accustomed to the movement patterns required for any specific system that you might use. This is usually called a *shadow drill*.

Shadow Drill

Play on a regulation-sized field with goals. Select the system to be used and position your teammates accordingly within one half of the field. Position your goalkeeper in the goal with a supply of soccer balls. The goalkeeper begins the exercise by distributing a ball to either a defender or a midfielder. From that point you and your teammates collectively pass the ball down the field and shoot it into the opposing goal. Do not involve any opponents in this exercise. Emphasize proper movement of all players in relation to the ball as you pass it down the field toward the goal. Players should return to their original positions after each score. Repeat the exercise 10 times, then move to the next system.

Success Goals =

9 out of 10 correct repetitions using the 4-2-4 system

9 out of 10 correct repetitions using the 4-4-2 system

9 out of 10 correct repetitions using the 4-3-3 system

9 out of 10 correct repetitions using the 3-5-2 system

Your Score =

(#) _____ correct 4-2-4 repetitions

(#) _____ correct 4-4-2 repetitions

(#) _____ correct 4-3-3 repetitions

(#) _____ correct 3-5-2 repetitions

Rating Your Total Progress

At this point you have been exposed to all of the basic skills used in actual game play as well as the strategies used on an individual, small group, and team basis. You are now ready to participate in and thoroughly enjoy the world's most popular team sport. It is my hope that you derive as much enjoyment and camaraderie from your soccer experiences as I have, that you continue to develop and improve as a player, and that you share your knowledge and expertise with those willing and eager to learn.

The following self-rating inventory is provided so you can judge your overall progress to this point. Read each item carefully and respond as objectively as possible.

PHYSICAL SKILLS

The first general success goal in a soccer course is to develop the physical skills needed to play the game. How would you rate yourself on the following skills?

	Very good	Good	Okay	Poor
Passing skills				
Inside of foot	_____	_____	_____	_____
Outside of foot	_____	_____	_____	_____
Instep	_____	_____	_____	_____
Short chip	_____	_____	_____	_____
Long chip	_____	_____	_____	_____
Receiving skills				
Inside of foot	_____	_____	_____	_____
Outside of foot	_____	_____	_____	_____
Instep	_____	_____	_____	_____
Thigh	_____	_____	_____	_____
Chest	_____	_____	_____	_____
Head	_____	_____	_____	_____

	Very good	Good	Okay	Poor
Dribbling and shielding skills				
Dribbling for control	_____	_____	_____	_____
Dribbling for speed	_____	_____	_____	_____
Shielding	_____	_____	_____	_____
Tackling skills				
Block tackle	_____	_____	_____	_____
Poke tackle	_____	_____	_____	_____
Slide tackle	_____	_____	_____	_____
Heading skills				
Jump header	_____	_____	_____	_____
Dive header	_____	_____	_____	_____
Shooting skills				
Instep drive	_____	_____	_____	_____
Full volley	_____	_____	_____	_____
Half volley	_____	_____	_____	_____
Side volley	_____	_____	_____	_____
Swerving shot	_____	_____	_____	_____
Goalkeeping skills				
Goalkeeper stance	_____	_____	_____	_____
Receiving a rolling ball	_____	_____	_____	_____
Receiving a ball to side	_____	_____	_____	_____
Receiving a medium-height ball	_____	_____	_____	_____
Receiving a chest-high ball	_____	_____	_____	_____
Receiving a high ball	_____	_____	_____	_____
Diving	_____	_____	_____	_____
Distributing by rolling	_____	_____	_____	_____
Distributing by baseball throw	_____	_____	_____	_____
Distributing by javelin throw	_____	_____	_____	_____
Distributing by punting	_____	_____	_____	_____

GAME STRATEGIES

The second general success goal in a soccer course is to develop an understanding of the strategies used on an individual, small group, and team basis. How would you rate your ability to use the following strategies in a game situation?

	Very good	Good	Okay	Poor
Individual attack				
Maintain ball possession	____	____	____	____
Create space for yourself	____	____	____	____
Turn on defender	____	____	____	____
Take on defender	____	____	____	____
Take shortest route to goal	____	____	____	____
Individual defense				
Control/balance	____	____	____	____
Approach to ball	____	____	____	____
Defensive stance	____	____	____	____
Marking distance	____	____	____	____
Goalside position	____	____	____	____
Preventing turn	____	____	____	____
Containment	____	____	____	____
Tackling the ball	____	____	____	____
Small group strategies in attack				
Give and go pass	____	____	____	____
Support positioning	____	____	____	____
Small group strategies in defense				
Cover	____	____	____	____
Balance	____	____	____	____
Attacking as a team				
Movement with and without the ball	____	____	____	____
Combination play	____	____	____	____
Improvisation	____	____	____	____
Team support	____	____	____	____
Finishing the attack	____	____	____	____
Defending as a team				
Immediate pressure	____	____	____	____
Fall back and delay	____	____	____	____

	Very good	Good	Okay	Poor
Limit space	———	———	———	———
Depth in defense	———	———	———	———
Deny space behind defense	———	———	———	———
Eliminate passing options	———	———	———	———
Make play predictable	———	———	———	———
Challenge for the ball	———	———	———	———

OVERALL SOCCER PROGRESS

Considering all the physical and strategical factors listed previously, how would you rate your overall progress?

____ Very successful

____ Successful

____ Fairly successful

____ Barely successful

____ Unsuccessful

ADDITIONAL COMMENTS AND QUESTIONS

Review your self-ratings. What were your strong points? What were your weaker points? How can you improve your performance? Are you willing to spend the time and effort needed to improve your game? Answering these questions will give you an idea of where you are and where you are going with respect to your soccer performance.

Individual Program

INDIVIDUAL COURSE IN _____ GRADE/COURSE SECTION _____

STUDENT'S NAME _____ STUDENT ID # _____

SKILLS/CONCEPTS	TECHNIQUE AND PERFORMANCE OBJECTIVES	WT* ×	POINT PROGRESS** =				FINAL SCORE***
			1	2	3	4	

Note. From "The Role of Expert Knowledge Structures in an Instructional Design Model for Physical Education" by J.N. Vickers, 1983, *Journal of Teaching in Physical Education*, **2**(3), p. 17. Copyright 1983 by Joan N. Vickers. Adapted by permission.

*WT = Weighting of an objective's degree of difficulty.

**PROGRESS = Ongoing success, which may be expressed in terms of (a) accumulated points (1, 2, 3, 4); (b) grades (D, C, B, A); (c) symbols (merit, bronze, silver, gold); (d) unsatisfactory/satisfactory; and others as desired.

***FINAL SCORE equals WT times PROGRESS.

Glossary

Attacker: The player with possession of the ball. Front running attackers are usually called strikers or wingers.

Balance in Defense: Positioning of defensive players that provides depth and support. Players nearest the ball mark opponents while those away from the ball position to cover space.

Ball-Watching: As a defender, focusing solely on the ball and losing sight of the opponent being marked; a common error among inexperienced players.

Baseball Throw: A method used by goalkeepers to toss the ball over medium distances.

Blindside Run: A type of running off-the-ball in which a player without the ball runs outside of the opponent's field of vision in order to receive a pass.

Block Tackle: A defensive skill used to gain possession of the ball; the player uses the inside of the foot to block the ball away from an opponent.

Breakaway: Situation where an attacker with the ball breaks free of defenders and creates a 1 versus 1 situation with the goalkeeper.

Concentration in Defense: Positioning of defensive players to limit the space available to opponents in the most critical scoring areas.

Counterattack: The initiation of an attack on the opposing goal upon gaining possession of the ball.

Cover: Defensive support. As a defender challenges for possession of the ball he or she should be supported from behind (covered) by a teammate.

Cross: A pass originating from the wing or flank area that is driven across the goal mouth.

Defenders: A general term used to label the players positioned nearest to the goalkeeper. Most modern systems of play use four defenders.

Depth: Proper support positioning of the team, both in attack and defense.

Diagonal Run: Run designed to penetrate the defense while drawing defenders away from central positions.

Direct Kick: A free kick that can be scored without first touching another player.

Economical Training: Incorporating fitness, skill, and tactics into each drill or exercise to make maximal use of practice time.

Far Post: The goal post farthest from the ball.

Flanks: Areas of the field near the touchlines that provide a narrow shooting angle to goal.

Forwards: Players who occupy the front attacking positions; usually identified as strikers and wingers.

Full Volley: Striking the ball directly out of the air, most commonly with the instep of the foot.

Functional Training: Isolating for practice the techniques and tactics of specific player positions (such as the skill used by a striker in receiving the ball when under pressure of an opponent).

Give and Go Pass: A combination pass with one player passing to a nearby teammate and then sprinting forward to receive a return pass.

Goalside Position: Defending player positioned between his or her goal and the opponent to be marked.

Grid: A confined area in which a small group of players practices skills and tactics.

Half Volley: Striking the ball dropping from above the instant it contacts the ground.

Indirect Kick: A free kick from which a goal cannot be scored directly. The ball must be touched by another player before entering the goal.

Marking: Tight coverage of an opponent.

Mobility: Movement both with and without the ball designed to create space for teammates by drawing opponents into unfavorable positions.

Near Post: The goal post nearest the ball.

Offside Rule: A player must have two opponents, including the goalkeeper, between himself or herself and the opposing goal at the moment the ball is played. Otherwise, he or she is offside and is penalized by an indirect free kick awarded to the opposing team. Players cannot be offside if they are positioned in their own half of the field, if the ball was last played by an opponent, or if they receive the ball directly from a corner kick, throw-in, goal kick, or drop ball.

One-on-One Defense: System in which each player is responsible for marking a specific opponent.

One-Touch Passing: Interpassing among teammates without stopping the ball; also called first-time passing.

Overlap: Method in which a supporting teammate runs from behind to a position ahead of the player with the ball; often used as a tactic to move defenders and midfielders into attacking positions.

Poke Tackle: A method in which a player reaches in and uses the toes to poke the ball away from an opponent.

Ready Position: The goalkeeper's basic stance when the ball is within shooting range of the goal.

Restart: A method of initiating play after a stop in the action. Restarts include direct and indirect free kicks, throw-ins, corner kicks, goal kicks, and the drop ball.

Running Off-the-Ball: Movement of a player without the ball that creates passing and scoring opportunities for teammates.

Shielding: Positioning one's body between the opponent and the ball to maintain possession.

Shoulder Charge: A legal tactic used when challenging an opponent for the ball when the ball is within playing distance.

Slide Tackle: A method in which a player slides and kicks the ball away from an opponent.

Stopper Back: A central defender positioned in front of the sweeper back who usually marks the opposing center striker.

Striker: A front-running forward positioned in the central area of the field; usually one of the primary goal scorers on the team.

Support: Movement of players into positions that provide passing options for the teammate with the ball.

Sweeper Back: The last field player in defense who provides cover for the marking defenders.

System of Play: Organization and responsibilities of the 10 field players.

Tactics: Organizational concept on an individual, group, or team basis of player roles within the team structure.

Techniques: Game skills which include passing and receiving, heading, dribbling, shooting, and shielding.

Throw-In: A method of restarting play after the ball has traveled outside the touchlines. The ball must be held with two hands and released directly over the head. Both feet must be touching the ground when the ball is released.

Touchline: A side boundary line.

Two-Touch Passing: Type of interpassing in which the receiving player controls the ball with the first touch and passes to a teammate on the second.

Wall Pass: A combination pass with one player serving as a barrier to redirect the path of the ball. The player in possession passes off the ''wall'' and immediately sprints forward into open space to receive the return pass.

Width in Attack: Using the width of the field in an attempt to draw defending players away from central positions. The objective is to create space in the most dangerous attacking zones.

Wingbacks: Defenders positioned on the flanks who usually mark the opposing wing forwards.

Winger: A front-running forward positioned in the flank area near the touchline.

Zonal Defense: System in which each player is responsible for defending a certain area of the field.

Joseph A. Luxbacher is a former professional player in the North American Soccer League (NASL), the American Soccer League (ASL), and the Major Indoor Soccer League (MISL). He coaches varsity soccer at the University of Pittsburgh and holds an ''A'' coaching license of the United States Soccer Federation. Dr. Luxbacher serves as a consultant at soccer camps and clinics throughout the eastern United States and is a codirector of Keystone Soccer Kamps. He has addressed various national and regional conventions, including The Olympic Symposium for Coaches, and has published articles on health and fitness, nutrition, outdoor recreation, and sport psychology and sport sociology.

Dr. Luxbacher holds a doctorate in health, physical, and recreation education and has published four previous books, including *The Soccer Goalkeeper* and *Fun Games for Soccer Training*. In his leisure, he enjoys tennis, hiking, and photography.